TWELFTH NIGHT

SPLIT LINES

Often, Shakespeare splits an iambic pentameter line across two or three speakers. In this book, both the original text and the retelling are indented to align with the continued sentence, highlighting this as a split line.

> **VIOLA**
> It gives a very echo to the seat
> *It gives a true reflection of the feeling*
>
> Where love is throned.
> *Of perfect love.*
>
> **ORSINO**
> Thou dost speak masterly.
> *You've called that perfectly.*

EXCEPTIONS

Two exceptions to the regular iambic pentameter format are widely used by Shakespeare:

1) Weak Endings
Regular iambic pentameter has 10 syllables, but an additional syllable can be added to create what is known as a 'weak ending'. Shakespeare's most famous line has a weak ending:

> *To be, or not to be? That is the question.*
> *The better part of valour is discretion.*
> *di-dum di-dum di-dum di-dum di-dum <u>di</u>*

2) Trochaic substitution
Though an iamb is 'di-dum', a trochee is 'dum-di',
> e.g. *biscuit, reason; bathroom.*

Replacing the first iamb with a trochee is known as 'trochaic substitution', e.g.,

> *Vaulting ambition, which o'erleaps itself.*
> *Now is the winter of our discontent.*
> <u>*dum-di*</u> *di-dum di-dum di-dum di-dum.*

VERSE VS PROSE

Not every line of Shakespeare's work is written in iambic pentameter. Often he simply wrote in prose, albeit embellished with poetic qualities. It's easy to tell the difference:

Verse: The first word of an iambic pentameter line is ALWAYS capitalised, even if it's a continuation of a sentence from the previous line.

Prose: Prose lines are not capitalised, unless the norms of sentence structure require it.

RHYME

Shakespeare often uses rhyme to emphasise the poetics of the line, especially to signify the closing lines of a particular scene. Throughout these retellings, the rhyme structure is followed (although not always using the same word Shakespeare used to rhyme with.)

CHARACTERS

VIOLA

After surviving a shipwreck, Viola finds herself washed up on the shores of Illyria. Fearing her brother has drowned, she seeks employment as a servant to Duke Orsino, requiring her to disguise as a man, called Cesario.

Olivia, who Duke Orsino has fallen in love with, falls for 'Cesario', whilst Viola – still disguised as Cesario – falls for Duke Orsino.

All seems lost until the surprise arrival of Viola's brother Sebastian to untangle the mess.

DUKE ORSINO

We find Duke Orsino suffering pangs of love for Olivia, a lady seemingly not interested in his advances.

Melancholy and despondent, he grows fond of his 'male' servant Cesario (Viola), who – unbeknownst to him – is a woman, and who has fallen for him.

It requires the revelation of identities to allow the relationship to flourish.

OLIVIA

Olivia is in mourning for her brother and will not entertain any thoughts of romance, rebuffing the amorous approaches of Duke Orsino.

However, when 'Cesario' approaches – Viola dressed as a man – she breaks her abstinence by falling for 'him'.

When all is revealed, the fickleness of her affection is reflected in her sudden acceptance of Duke Orsino.

MALVOLIO

The pompous head servant to Lady Olivia, he wins no friends amongst his peers by his haughty arrogance.

However, his world is turned upside down when he receives a note believing to be from his mistress Lady Olivia, supposedly declaring her love for him. A trick by Toby and Sir Andrew, Malvolio is dispelled to a cell, deeming him to be mad.

When all is revealed, he vows a shallow revenge on his perpetrators.

SIR TOBY BELCH

The uncouth uncle of Lady Olivia, Sir Toby Belch enjoys excessive boozing and debauchery with his dim-witted friend Sir Andrew Aguecheek.

Together with Olivia's maid Maria, they hatch a plan to trick Malvolio into thinking his mistress loves him, leading Malvolio to shame and ruin.

SIR ANDREW AGUECHEEK

A wet and idiotic man, friends with Sir Toby, who thinks he has a chance of love with Lady Olivia.

He gets in an unwanted fight, only to be taken on by Antonio, who thinks he's fighting his friend Sebastian.

MARIA

Olivia's rambunctious maid, she aligns with Sir Toby and Sir Andrew to formulate a plan to trick and bring down the pompous Malvolio.

FABIAN

Another foolish friend of Sir Toby and Sir Andrew, Fabian is central to the wind up of Malvolio and a stirrer in the fight with Cesario.

SEBASTIAN

Viola believes her brother Sebastian died in the storm she survived. But when Sebastian shows up in town with his dear friend Antonio, his exact likeness to his twin sister causes confusion.

Initially bemused by the advances of Olivia – who thinks he's Cesario – he quickly weakens and marries the noble lady without resistance.

When Sir Andrew starts to fight the timid Cesario, he gets a shock when Sebastian appears with a step-change level of aggression.

ANTONIO

Friends with Sebastian, Antonio's past battles with Duke Orsino come back to haunt him, as he is arrested when attempting to fight Sir Andrew.

He latterly meets Viola, believing it to be Sebastian, and is dumbfounded that his 'friend' disowns him in his time of need.

FESTE

Lady Olivia's jester Feste provides light relief and irritation in equal measure, winding up the protagonists with riddles and jokes, songs and dances.

Despite his role as a clown, he often seems wiser than most other characters in the play.

ACT 1

ACT 1, SCENE 1

DUKE ORSINO'S PALACE.

[ENTER DUKE ORSINO, CURIO, AND OTHER LORDS; MUSICIANS ATTENDING]

DUKE ORSINO
If music be the food of love, play on;
If music is the fuel of love, play on!
Give me excess of it, that, surfeiting,
Play tunes aplenty till I've heard too much,
The appetite may sicken, and so die.
And then these pangs will pale and fade away.
That strain again! It had a dying fall:
Play that refrain again; I found it haunting.
O, it came o'er my ear like the sweet sound,   5
To me, it sounded like the gentle purr
That breathes upon a bank of violets,
Of blowing breeze through violets on a bank,
Stealing and giving odour! Enough; no more:
Distributing their scent. But, that's enough!
'Tis not so sweet now as it was before.
For now, love's not as sweet as once it was.
O spirit of love! How quick and fresh art thou,
Oh love, one moment you are fresh and racy,
That, notwithstanding thy capacity   10
And even though you have capacity
Receiveth as the sea, nought enters there,
To drink all water from the sea, you don't,
Of what validity and pitch soe'er,
Despite how fine and wonderful it is;
But falls into abatement and low price,
You let your thirst decline and fade away

1

Even in a minute: so full of shapes is fancy
In just a minute. Love is always changing

That it alone is high fantastical.   15
And that's fantastically magnificent.

CURIO
Will you go hunt, my lord?
My lord, are you off hunting?

DUKE ORSINO
What, Curio?
Hunting what?

CURIO
The hart.
The stag.

DUKE ORSINO
Why, so I do, the noblest that I have:
Oh yes, I'll hunt the finest heart there is.

O, when mine eyes did see Olivia first,   20
For when my eyes first saw Olivia,

Methought she purged the air of pestilence!
I thought she cleansed the air of all disease.

That instant was I turned into a hart;
And from that moment I became a stag,

And my desires, like fell and cruel hounds,
And my desires, akin to savage hounds,

E'er since pursue me.
Have hounded me since then.

[ENTER VALENTINE]

              How now! What news from her?   25
              Hi, what's she said?

VALENTINE
So please my lord, I might not be admitted;
Apologies, my lord, I didn't see her,

But from her handmaid do return this answer:
But got this answer for you from her maid:

The element itself, till seven years' heat,
The sun itself, for seven summers more,

Shall not behold her face at ample view;
Won't get to see her unobstructed face,

But, like a cloistress, she will veiled walk   30
Because she'll wear a veil like a nun,

And water once a day her chamber round
And cry each day as she walks round her bedroom

With eye-offending brine: all this to season
With stinging tears, for only to preserve

A brother's dead love, which she would keep fresh
The love for her dead brother, which she'll keep

And lasting in her sad remembrance.
Alive in her sad memories of him.

DUKE ORSINO
O, she that hath a heart of that fine frame   35
If she has such a noble-minded heart

To pay this debt of love but to a brother,
That pays this debt of love just to her brother,

How will she love, when the rich golden shaft
Imagine how she'll love when Cupid's arrow

Hath killed the flock of all affections else
Has killed off all those sources of affection

That live in her; when liver, brain and heart,
That she has now; when all her vital organs,

These sovereign thrones, are all supplied, and filled   40
That govern how she loves, all overwhelm

Her sweet perfections with one self king!
Her sweet perfections with the love of me!

Away before me to sweet beds of flowers:
Lead me away to lie amongst sweet flowers;

Love-thoughts lie rich when canopied with bowers.
For plants give thoughts of love far greater powers.

[EXEUNT]

ACT 1, SCENE 2

THE SEA-COAST.

[ENTER VIOLA, A CAPTAIN, AND SAILORS]

VIOLA
What country, friends, is this?
What country, friends, is this?

CAPTAIN
This is Illyria, lady.
This is Illyria, lady.

VIOLA
And what should I do in Illyria?
Illyria? What am I doing here?
My brother he is in Elysium.
My brother's in Elysium, our heaven.
Perchance he is not drowned: what think you, sailors?   5
Perhaps he hasn't drowned. What do you think, crew?

CAPTAIN
It is perchance that you yourself were saved.
It was just down to luck that you were saved.

VIOLA
O my poor brother! And so perchance may he be.
Oh, my poor brother! There's a chance he lived.

CAPTAIN
True, madam: and, to comfort you with chance,
That's true, and drawing comfort from that chance,
Assure yourself, after our ship did split,
You must know, once our ship disintegrated,
When you and those poor number saved with you   10
When you and those few others that survived
Hung on our driving boat, I saw your brother,
Clung to our drifting raft, I saw your brother,

Most provident in peril, bind himself,
  With foresight in the danger, tie himself—
Courage and hope both teaching him the practise,
  As bravery and optimism taught him—
To a strong mast that lived upon the sea;
  To a strong mast that floated on the sea,
Where, like Arion on the dolphin's back,   15
  Where, like Arion rode the dolphin's back,
I saw him hold acquaintance with the waves
  He held his own, buoyant above the waves,
So long as I could see.
  As long as I could see.

VIOLA
For saying so, there's gold:
  For saying that, here's money.
Mine own escape unfoldeth to my hope,
  That I survived gives hope that he did too,
Whereto thy speech serves for authority,   20
  And what you said affirms this could be true
The like of him. Know'st thou this country?
  And he survived. Do you know of this country?

CAPTAIN
Ay, madam, well; for I was bred and born
  I know it well, for I was born and raised
Not three hours' travel from this very place.
  Less than three hours journey-time from here.

VIOLA
Who governs here?
  Who governs here?

CAPTAIN
A noble duke, in nature as in name.   25
  A noble duke, in nature and in name.

VIOLA
What is the name?
  What is his name?

5

CAPTAIN
Orsino.
  Orsino.

VIOLA
Orsino! I have heard my father name him:
  Orsino? Hmm. My father mentioned him.

He was a bachelor then.
  He used to be a bachelor back then.

CAPTAIN
And so is now, or was so very late;   30
  And still he is, at least last time I checked;

For but a month ago I went from hence,
  But, just a month ago when leaving here,

And then 'twas fresh in murmur,--as, you know,
  I heard a rumour—people like to gossip

What great ones do the less will prattle of,--
  About the goings-on of royalty—

That he did seek the love of fair Olivia.
  That he desired to win Olivia's heart.

VIOLA
What's she?   35
  Who's she?

CAPTAIN
A virtuous maid, the daughter of a count
  A pristine maid, the daughter of a count

That died some twelvemonth since, then leaving her
  Who died a year ago, thus leaving her

In the protection of his son, her brother,
  To be protected by his son, her brother,

Who shortly also died: for whose dear love,
  But he soon died as well, and for his love,

They say, she hath abjured the company   40
  They say, she has forgone the sight of men

And sight of men.
  And won't be seen with them.

6

VIOLA

O that I served that lady
Oh, how I'd like to be that lady's maid,

And might not be delivered to the world,
And not reveal my status to the world—

Till I had made mine own occasion mellow,
Until my own position has matured—

What my estate is! 45
To show them who I am.

CAPTAIN

That were hard to compass;
That will be tough

Because she will admit no kind of suit,
For she will not hear any such request,

No, not the duke's.
Not even from the Duke.

VIOLA

There is a fair behaviour in thee, captain;
You seem to be a decent person, captain,

And though that nature with a beauteous wall 50
And though in nature things that look delightful

Doth oft close in pollution, yet of thee
Can often hide a nasty trait, but you

I will believe thou hast a mind that suits
Possess, I think, a disposition matched with

With this thy fair and outward character.
Your kind and generous outward character.

I prithee, and I'll pay thee bounteously,
I beg you—and I'll pay you handsomely—

Conceal me what I am, and be my aid 55
Help me conceal myself and help me find

For such disguise as haply shall become
A suitable disguise to match the will

The form of my intent. I'll serve this duke:
Of whom I want to be. I'll serve this duke.

Thou shall present me as an eunuch to him:
You'll introduce me as a eunuch to him.

It may be worth thy pains; for I can sing
It will be worth your while, for I can sing

And speak to him in many sorts of music   60
And play to him all different kinds of music

That will allow me very worth his service.
And thereby justify my service to him.

What else may hap to time I will commit;
Whatever else may happen, time will tell,

Only shape thou thy silence to my wit.
But you must keep my secret safe as well.

CAPTAIN
Be you his eunuch, and your mute I'll be:
You'll be his eunuch; I won't say word.

When my tongue blabs, then let mine eyes not see.   65
Let me go blind if from my mouth it's heard.

VIOLA
I thank thee: lead me on.
I thank you. Lead me on.

[EXEUNT]

ACT 1, SCENE 3

OLIVIA'S HOUSE.

[ENTER SIR TOBY BELCH AND MARIA]

SIR TOBY BELCH
What a plague means my niece, to take the death of
Why does my niece lament her brother's death

her brother thus? I am sure care's an enemy to life.
as though it were the plague? It can't be healthy.

MARIA
By my troth, Sir Toby, you must come in earlier o'
Sir Toby, in God's name, come back here sooner

nights: your cousin, my lady, takes great
each night. Your cousin, to whom I'm maid, dislikes

exceptions to your ill hours.   5
you staying out so late.

SIR TOBY BELCH
Why, let her except, before excepted.
I take exception to her flawed exception!

MARIA
Ay, but you must confine yourself within the modest
Yes, but you should conduct yourself within

limits of order.
the confines of acceptable behaviour.

SIR TOBY BELCH
Confine! I'll confine myself no finer than I am:
Confines? I'm only confined by my clothing.

these clothes are good enough to drink in; and so be   10
These clothes are good enough to drink in; also

these boots too: an they be not, let them hang
these boots are too. And if they're not, they'll hang

9

themselves in their own straps.
themselves by their own laces!

MARIA
That quaffing and drinking will undo you: I heard
Your bingeing drunkenness will be your downfall.
my lady talk of it yesterday; and of a foolish
Just yesterday, she mentioned it and also
knight that you brought in one night here   15
spoke of a foolish knight you once brought home
to be her wooer.
to chat her up.

SIR TOBY BELCH
Who, Sir Andrew Aguecheek?
Who? Sir Andrew Aguecheek?

MARIA
Ay, he.
Yes, him.

SIR TOBY BELCH
He's as tall a man as any's in Illyria.
He's tall as any man here in Illyria.

MARIA
What's that to the purpose?   20
What's that got to do with it?

SIR TOBY BELCH
Why, he has three thousand ducats a year.
He earns three thousand ducats every year!

MARIA
Ay, but he'll have but a year in all these ducats:
Yes, but he loses all of them each year.
he's a very fool and a prodigal.
He's foolish with his money, over-lavish.

SIR TOBY BELCH
Fie, that you'll say so! He plays o' the
Go wash your mouth with soap! For he can play
viol-de-gamboys, and speaks three or four languages   25
the cello, and speaks three or four languages

word for word without book, and hath all the good
without a dictionary, and has been blessed

gifts of nature.
with natural talent.

MARIA
He hath indeed, almost natural: for besides that
He has been blessed indeed, because not only

he's a fool, he's a great quarreller: and but that
is he a fool, he's argumentative,

he hath the gift of a coward to allay the gust he   30
and if he wasn't also such a coward

hath in quarrelling, 'tis thought among the prudent
when arguing with gusto, it's been said

he would quickly have the gift of a grave.
somebody would have put him in his grave.

SIR TOBY BELCH
By this hand, they are scoundrels and subtractors
I tell you, they are lowlife criticisers

that say so of him. Who are they?
that speak of him like that. Tell me, who are they?

MARIA
They that add, moreover, he's drunk nightly in your
company.   35
Those folk who say he's drunk each night with you.

SIR TOBY BELCH
With drinking healths to my niece: I'll drink to
By drinking toasts to my dear niece. I'll toast her

her as long as there is a passage in my throat and
as long as there's a passage in my throat and

drink in Illyria: he's a coward and a coystrill
Illyria has drink. What cowardly scumbag

that will not drink to my niece till his brains turn   40
won't toast my niece until his brains are spinning

o' the toe like a parish-top. What, wench!
just like a spinning-top, hey wench?

Castiliano vulgo! For here comes Sir Andrew Agueface.
Eh up! Here comes Sir Andrew Agueface right now!

11

[ENTER SIR ANDREW]

SIR ANDREW
Sir Toby Belch! How now, Sir Toby Belch!
Sir Toby Belch! What's up, Sir Toby Belch?

SIR TOBY BELCH
Sweet Sir Andrew!
My dear Sir Andrew!

SIR ANDREW
Bless you, fair shrew.   45
Bless you, my pretty mouse.

MARIA
And you too, sir.
And you too, sir.

SIR TOBY BELCH
Accost, Sir Andrew, accost.
Go chat her up, Sir Andrew! Chat her up!

SIR ANDREW
What's that?
Who is she?

SIR TOBY BELCH
My niece's chambermaid.
My niece's chambermaid.

SIR ANDREW
Good Mistress Accost, I desire better   50
Good Mistress Chatterup, I'd like to get
acquaintance.
to know you better.

MARIA
My name is Mary, sir.
My name is Mary, sir.

SIR ANDREW
Good Mistress Mary Accost,--
Good Mistress Mary Chatterup...

SIR TOBY BELCH
You mistake, knight; 'accost' is front her, board
You've got this wrong, dear boy. By 'chat her up',

12

her, woo her, assail her. 55
I mean seduce her, woo her, kiss her...shag her!

SIR ANDREW
By my troth, I would not undertake her in this
Good gracious, I would not do that to her

company. Is that the meaning of 'accost'?
in front of you. Is that what 'Chatterup' means?

MARIA
Fare you well, gentlemen.
Goodbye, gentlemen.

SIR TOBY BELCH
An thou let part so, Sir Andrew, would thou mightst
If you just let her leave like this, Sir Andrew,

never draw sword again. 60
you don't deserve to draw your sword again.

SIR ANDREW
An you part so, mistress, I would I might never
If you just leave, my dear, I don't deserve

draw sword again. Fair lady, do you think you have
to draw my sword again. Good lady, do you

fools in hand?
think that your hands are full of fools?

MARIA
Sir, I have not you by the hand.
Sir, I don't have you by the hand.

SIR ANDREW
Marry, but you shall have; and here's my hand. 65
Indeed you don't, not yet; but here's my hand.

MARIA
Now, sir, 'thought is free:' I pray you, bring
Now sir, I am entitled to opinions.

your hand to the buttery-bar and let it drink.
I urge you, wet your hands here at the bar.

SIR ANDREW
Wherefore, sweet-heart? What's your metaphor?
What for, sweetheart? What do you really mean?

MARIA
It's dry, sir.
Sir, just my dry humour.

SIR ANDREW
Why, I think so: I am not such an ass but I can   70
Well, I think so. I'm not so stupid that

keep my hand dry. But what's your jest?
my hands get wet by rain. But what's the joke?

MARIA
A dry jest, sir.
Sir, just a dry joke.

SIR ANDREW
Are you full of them?
Do you have many jokes?

MARIA
Ay, sir, I have them at my fingers' ends:
Yes, sir, they're at the tip of every finger.

marry, now I let go your hand, I am barren.   75
But letting go of you, my jokes are gone.

[EXIT]

SIR TOBY BELCH
O knight thou lackest a cup of canary: when did I
Dear boy, you need Canary Island wine!

see thee so put down?
When have I ever seen you so outwitted?

SIR ANDREW
Never in your life, I think; unless you see canary
You never have, except when I was drunk by

put me down. Methinks sometimes I have no more wit
too much Canary wine. I sometimes think

than a Christian or an ordinary man has: but I am a   80
I am no smarter than a simple Christian.

great eater of beef and I believe that does harm to my wit.
But, also, I eat beef, and that dulls one's wit.

SIR TOBY BELCH
No question.
No question.

SIR ANDREW
An I thought that, I'ld forswear it.
I'd give it up if I really believed that.
I'll ride home to-morrow, Sir Toby.
Tomorrow, I'll be riding home, Sir Toby.

SIR TOBY BELCH
Pourquoi, my dear knight?   85
Pourquoi, my dear knight?

SIR ANDREW
What is 'Pourquoi'? Do or not do? I would I had
What does 'pourquoi' mean? Should I? Should I not?
bestowed that time in the tongues that I have in
I wish I'd spent more time rehearsing language
fencing, dancing and bear-baiting:
as I did fencing, dancing, bearbaiting.
O, had I but followed the arts!
I should have studied arts!

SIR TOBY BELCH
Then hadst thou had an excellent head of hair.   90
If so, you'd have a lovely head of hair.

SIR ANDREW
Why, would that have mended my hair?
Why, would that then have rectified my hair?

SIR TOBY BELCH
Past question; for thou seest it will not curl by nature.
Without a doubt; it won't curl on its own.

SIR ANDREW
But it becomes me well enough, does't not?
It doesn't look too bad though, does it not?

SIR TOBY BELCH
Excellent; it hangs like flax on a distaff; and I
Divine! Like wool spun on a spinning shaft;
hope to see a housewife take thee between her legs   95
I hope you get between a slapper's legs

15

and spin it off.
and that she spins it off to turn you bald.

SIR ANDREW
Faith, I'll home to-morrow, Sir Toby: your niece
Sir Toby, I'll be going home tomorrow.

will not be seen; or if she be, it's four to one
I'll never see your niece, or if I do,

she'll none of me: the count himself here hard by woos her.
she won't see me. The Count wants to seduce her.

SIR TOBY BELCH
She'll none o' the count: she'll not match above   *100*
She won't go with the Count. She's not attracted

her degree, neither in estate, years, nor wit;
to smarter, richer, older, funnier men.

I have heard her swear't. Tut, there's life in't, man.
I heard her swear it; you've still got a chance.

SIR ANDREW
I'll stay a month longer. I am a fellow o' the
I'll stay another month. I am a chap with

strangest mind i' the world; I delight in masques
the world's most unique mind. I love displays

and revels sometimes altogether.   *105*
of dancing, merriment; sometimes, together.

SIR TOBY BELCH
Art thou good at these kickshawses, knight?
Are you good at those fun frivolities?

SIR ANDREW
As any man in Illyria, whatsoever he be, under the
As good as any man here in Illyria...

degree of my betters; and yet I will not compare
...except, of course, by those better than me...

with an old man.
...or those ones who have done it more than me.

SIR TOBY BELCH
What is thy excellence in a galliard, knight?   *110*
How good are you at hot-step dance, then knight?

SIR ANDREW
Faith, I can cut a caper.
I tell you, I can really cut the mustard.

SIR TOBY BELCH
And I can cut the mutton to't.
And I can cut the mutton with it too.

SIR ANDREW
And I think I have the back-trick simply as strong
And I can do the backward kick as well

as any man in Illyria.
as any man here in Illyria.

SIR TOBY BELCH
Wherefore are these things hid? Wherefore have   *115*
Why do you hide these skills? Why close a curtain

these gifts a curtain before 'em? Are they like to
around these gifts you have? Should they be getting

take dust, like Mistress Mall's picture? Why dost
all dusty, like that painting? Why not go

thou not go to church in a galliard and come home in
to church doing the hot-step, then return

a coranto? My very walk should be a jig; I would not
by skipping? I would dance instead of walking.

so much as make water but in a sink-a-pace.   *120*
I'd even take a piss doing the five-step!

What dost thou mean? Is it a world to hide virtues in?
What are you thinking? Why d'you hide your skills?

I did think, by the excellent constitution of thy leg,
I thought that, judging by your shapely leg,

it was formed under the star of a galliard.
it had been born below a dancing star.

SIR ANDREW
Ay, 'tis strong, and it does indifferent well in a
Oh yes, it's strong, and it looks rather fine

flame-coloured stock. Shall we set about some revels?   *125*
in chestnut-coloured stockings. Shall we dance?

SIR TOBY BELCH
What shall we do else? Were we not born under Taurus?
What else is there to do? Weren't we born Taurus?

SIR ANDREW
Taurus! That's sides and heart.
Of Taurus? That one governs sides and heart.

SIR TOBY BELCH
No, sir; it is legs and thighs. Let me see the
No, sir: it governs legs and thighs. Let's dance.

caper; ha! Higher: ha, ha! Excellent!
Ha, higher! Ha, ha, you are excellent!

[EXEUNT]

ACT 1, SCENE 4

DUKE ORSINO'S PALACE.

[ENTER VALENTINE AND VIOLA IN MAN'S ATTIRE]

VALENTINE
If the duke continue these favours towards you,
  If Duke Orsino keeps on being nice
Cesario, you are like to be much advanced: he hath
  to you, Cesario, you'll get promoted.
known you but three days, and already you are no stranger.
  He's only known you three days, but he likes you.

VIOLA
You either fear his humour or my negligence, that
  You either think he's fickle or I'll screw up
you call in question the continuance of his love: 5
  because you doubt his love will carry on.
is he inconstant, sir, in his favours?
  Is he erratic with the folk he likes?

VALENTINE
No, believe me.
  Oh no, believe me.

VIOLA
I thank you. Here comes the count.
  Thank you. Here's the Duke.

[ENTER DUKE ORSINO, CURIO, AND ATTENDANTS]

DUKE ORSINO
Who saw Cesario, ho?
  Who's seen Cesario, then?

VIOLA

On your attendance, my lord; here. 10

I'm waiting for you here, my lord.

DUKE ORSINO

Stand you a while aloof, Cesario,

Wait there where you can't hear. Cesario,

Thou know'st no less but all; I have unclasped

You know the all of me. I have revealed

To thee the book even of my secret soul:

To you the very secrets of my soul.

Therefore, good youth, address thy gait unto her;

And so, young man, go take yourself to her

Be not denied access, stand at her doors, 15

And don't be turned away. Stand at her doors

And tell them, there thy fixed foot shall grow

And tell them that you will not budge an inch

Till thou have audience.

Until you've seen her.

VIOLA

                    Sure, my noble lord,

Surely though, my lord,

If she be so abandoned to her sorrow

If she's completely overwhelmed with grief,

As it is spoke, she never will admit me. 20

As people say, she won't invite me in.

DUKE ORSINO

Be clamorous and leap all civil bounds

Be blatantly obnoxious, out of order,

Rather than make unprofited return.

Instead of coming back without reply.

VIOLA

Say I do speak with her, my lord, what then?

And if I speak to her, what should I say?

DUKE ORSINO

O, then unfold the passion of my love,

Well, then reveal the passion of my heart.

20

Surprise her with discourse of my dear faith: 25
  Surprise her by disclosing I'm besotted.

It shall become thee well to act my woes;
  You will do well to show how much I'm suffering.

She will attend it better in thy youth
  She'll hear it better coming from a youngster

Than in a nuncio's of more grave aspect.
  Than from a messenger who's growing old.

VIOLA
I think not so, my lord.
  I don't think so, my lord.

DUKE ORSINO
              Dear lad, believe it; 30
              Dear lad, believe it,

For they shall yet belie thy happy years,
  For they'll misrepresent your youthful looks

That say thou art a man: Diana's lip
  By calling you a man. Diana's lips

Is not more smooth and rubious; thy small pipe
  Are not as smooth and red as yours; your voice

Is as the maiden's organ, shrill and sound,
  Is like a young girl's voice, high-pitched and shrill,

And all is semblative a woman's part. 35
  And all the rest of you looks feminine.

I know thy constellation is right apt
  I know your nature, set by stars, is right

For this affair. Some four or five attend him;
  To do this job. Go, four or five of you,

All, if you will; for I myself am best
  Or all if you prefer, for I am best

When least in company. Prosper well in this,
  When left alone. If you do well at this,

And thou shalt live as freely as thy lord, 40
  Then you shall live as freely as your lord,

To call his fortunes thine.
  And all my fortune's yours.

21

VIOLA

I'll do my best

I'll do my best

To woo your lady:

To woo your lady.

[Aside]

yet, a barful strife!

Oh, conflicted strife!

Whoe'er I woo, myself would be his wife.   45

I'll woo her, but I hope to be his wife.

[EXEUNT]

ACT 1, SCENE 5

OLIVIA'S HOUSE.

[ENTER MARIA AND CLOWN]

MARIA

Nay, either tell me where thou hast been, or I will
No, either tell me where you've been, or I

not open my lips so wide as a bristle may enter in
will keep my lips shut, and I won't defend you.

way of thy excuse: my lady will hang thee for thy absence.
My lady's going to hang you for your absence.

CLOWN

Let her hang me: he that is well hanged in this
Let her hang me, for he that is well hung

world needs to fear no colours.   5
has nothing left to fear.

MARIA

Make that good.
How do you mean?

CLOWN

He shall see none to fear.
When dead, you can't be scared.

MARIA

A good lenten answer: I can tell thee where that
A thin, pathetic answer. I can tell you

saying was born, of 'I fear no colours'.
where that phrase comes from, "nothing left to fear".

CLOWN

Where, good Mistress Mary?   10
From where, good Mistress Mary?

MARIA
In the wars; and that may you be bold to say in your foolery.
From war; but you don't know that as a fool.

CLOWN
Well, God give them wisdom that have it; and those
Well, God give further wisdom to the wise,

that are fools, let them use their talents.
and let the fools be foolish as they can be.

MARIA
Yet you will be hanged for being so long absent; or,
But you'll be hanged for being gone so long.

to be turned away, is not that as good as a hanging to you? 15
Or fired from your job, and that's the same, right?

CLOWN
Many a good hanging prevents a bad marriage; and,
Many bad marriages are saved by hanging,

for turning away, let summer bear it out.
and if I'm fired, I'll while away the summer.

MARIA
You are resolute, then?
You're dead-set, then?

CLOWN
Not so, neither; but I am resolved on two points.
Not dead-set, but I'm certain of two points.

MARIA
That if one break, the other will hold; or, if both   20
That if one of your braces breaks, one holds;

break, your gaskins fall.
but if both break, your pantaloons fall down?

CLOWN
Apt, in good faith; very apt. Well, go thy way; if
Touché, you said that well. Now, shuffle off.

Sir Toby would leave drinking, thou wert as witty a
If there's a day Sir Toby quits the booze,

piece of Eve's flesh as any in Illyria.
you'll be Illyria's funniest lady.

MARIA

Peace, you rogue, no more o' that. Here comes my   25
Shut up, you goon, I've heard enough. Here comes

lady: make your excuse wisely, you were best.
my lady. Do your best with your excuses.

[EXIT]

CLOWN

Wit, an't be thy will, put me into good fooling!
So, come on wit, give me some funny gags.

Those wits, that think they have thee, do very oft
Those smart folk that so often think they're funny

prove fools; and I, that am sure I lack thee, may
turn out to be the fools, and I'm not funny

pass for a wise man: for what says Quinapalus?   30
so they might think I'm wise. How goes the saying?

'Better a witty fool, than a foolish wit.'
"Better a witty fool than a foolish wit."

[ENTER OLIVIA WITH MALVOLIO]

God bless thee, lady!
God bless you, lady!

OLIVIA

Take the fool away.
Take the fool away.

CLOWN

Do you not hear, fellows? Take away the lady.
You heard her gentleman: remove the lady.

OLIVIA

Go to, you're a dry fool; I'll no more of you: 35
Clear off, you dry old fool. I'm done with you.

besides, you grow dishonest.
Besides, you're now dishonest.

CLOWN

Two faults, madonna, that drink and good counsel
Madonna, there are two faults that drink and guidance

will amend: for give the dry fool drink, then is
will overcome. With drink, a dry old fool's

25

the fool not dry: bid the dishonest man mend
no longer dry. Ask the dishonest man

himself; if he mend, he is no longer dishonest;   40
to mend his ways; if so, he's not dishonest;

if he cannot, let the botcher mend him. Any thing
if no, we'll let the tailor patch him up.

that's mended is but patched: virtue that
Things fixed are patched; for when somebody good

transgresses is but patched with sin; and sin that
does wrong, they're patched with sin, and when a sinner

amends is but patched with virtue. If that this
does good, he's patched with good. If these two statements

simple syllogism will serve, so; if it will not,   45
are right, then so be it. If not, what shall

what remedy? As there is no true cuckold but
we do? When someone's wife has been unfaithful,

calamity, so beauty's a flower. The lady bade take
that's trouble, like a flower approaching winter.

away the fool; therefore, I say again, take her away.
So, as the lady said, remove the fool.

OLIVIA
Sir, I bade them take away you.
It's you I told them all to take away.

CLOWN
Misprision in the highest degree! Lady, cucullus non   50
Injustice at its worst! Wearing a cloak

facit monachum; that's as much to say as I wear not
does not make you a monk. That's just the same

motley in my brain. Good madonna, give me leave to
as me not wearing costumes in my mind.

prove you a fool.
Madonna, let me prove you are a fool.

OLIVIA
Can you do it?
Can you do that?

CLOWN

Dexterously, good madonna.   55
  With great dexterity, my good madonna.

OLIVIA

Make your proof.
  Go on then, prove it.

CLOWN

I must catechise you for it, madonna: good my mouse
  I must cross-question you, madonna. Answer

of virtue, answer me.
  my questions, like a well-intentioned mouse.

OLIVIA

Well, sir, for want of other idleness, I'll bide your proof.
  For lack of something better, I will listen.

CLOWN

Good madonna, why mournest thou?   60
  Madonna, tell me why you are in mourning?

OLIVIA

Good fool, for my brother's death.
  Because my brother's dead, you fool.

CLOWN

I think his soul is in hell, madonna.
  I think his soul's in hell, my good madonna.

OLIVIA

I know his soul is in heaven, fool.
  I know his soul resides in heaven, fool.

CLOWN

The more fool, madonna, to mourn for your brother's
  Then you're the fool, madonna, for you're mourning

soul being in heaven. Take away the fool, gentlemen.   65
  your brother's soul in heaven. Take the fool, gents!

OLIVIA

What think you of this fool, Malvolio? Doth he not mend?
  Do you think this fool gets funnier, Malvolio?

MALVOLIO
Yes, and shall do till the pangs of death shake him:
I do, and he'll get funnier with age,

infirmity, that decays the wise, doth ever make the
until he dies. Old age degrades the wise

better fool.
but makes the fools more funny.

CLOWN
God send you, sir, a speedy infirmity, for the   70
God send you hastily to old age, sir,

better increasing your folly! Sir Toby will be
for then you might be funny. And Sir Toby

sworn that I am no fox; but he will not pass his
is sure that I'm not crafty, but there's no way

word for two pence that you are no fool.
that he won't bet against that you're a fool.

OLIVIA
How say you to that, Malvolio?
What do you say to that, Malvolio?

MALVOLIO
I marvel your ladyship takes delight in such a   75
My Lady, I'm amazed you take enjoyment

barren rascal: I saw him put down the other day
from this unfunny twerp. I saw him flummoxed

with an ordinary fool that has no more brain
the other day by a pathetic fool

than a stone. Look you now, he's out of his guard
whose brain was made of stone. He's given up

already; unless you laugh and minister occasion to
already. And unless you line his gags up,

him, he is gagged. I protest, I take these wise men,   80
he's stumped. I take these wise men that are laughing

that crow so at these set kind of fools, no better
at these pre-scripted jokes as nothing better

than the fools' zanies.
than sidekicks of the Jester.

28

OLIVIA

Oh, you are sick of self-love, Malvolio, and taste
You are so vain, Malvolio, you're tainted

with a distempered appetite. To be generous,
by poisoned taste. To be more kind and generous,

guiltless and of free disposition, is to take those   85
with open mind, just take the things he says

things for bird-bolts that you deem cannon-bullets:
as pops to scare the birds, not cannon fire.

there is no slander in an allowed fool, though he do
The words are not offensive from a fool,

nothing but rail; nor no railing in a known discreet
although he prattles on; and there's no prattling

man, though he do nothing but reprove.
from wise men who do nothing but chastise.

CLOWN

Now Mercury endue thee with leasing, for thou   90
Now may the god of cheating help you lie,

speakest well of fools!
for you are talking fondly of the fools!

[RE-ENTER MARIA]

MARIA

Madam, there is at the gate a young gentleman much
My lady, a young gentleman's arrived

desires to speak with you.
and he is very keen to speak to you.

OLIVIA

From the Count Orsino, is it?
Has he been sent by Count Orsino, then?

MARIA

I know not, madam: 'tis a fair young man, and well
attended.   95
I don't know. He's attractive, and there are others with him.

OLIVIA

Who of my people hold him in delay?
Which of my staff are keeping him at bay?

MARIA
Sir Toby, madam, your kinsman.
Your relative, Sir Toby, madam.

OLIVIA
Fetch him off, I pray you; he speaks nothing but madman:
Oh, stop him, please! He's always talking nonsense.

fie on him!
Just shove him off!

[EXIT MARIA]

Go you, Malvolio: if it be a suit from the count,   100
Go check, Malvolio. If it's a message from the Count,

I am sick, or not at home; what you will, to dismiss it.
I'm sick, or out; get rid of him somehow.

[EXIT MALVOLIO]

Now you see, sir, how your fooling grows old, and
Now look, sir, you must notice how your jesting

people dislike it.
is wearing thin and irritating people.

CLOWN
Thou hast spoke for us, madonna, as if thy eldest
You praise fools like you'd want your eldest son

son should be a fool; whose skull Jove cram with brains!   105
to be a fool! Thank goodness he is brainy,

For,--here he comes,--one of thy kin has a
for—here he comes—your relative most lacking

most weak pia mater.
in basic intellect.

[ENTER SIR TOBY BELCH]

OLIVIA
By mine honour, half drunk. What is he at the gate, cousin?
Good gracious, you're half drunk! Who's at the door?

SIR TOBY BELCH
A gentleman.
A gentleman.

OLIVIA
A gentleman! What gentleman?   *110*
A gentleman? What gentleman?

SIR TOBY BELCH
'Tis a gentle man here--a plague o' these
A gentleman is there. Those pickled herrings

pickle-herring! How now, sot!
have made me sick! How are you, silly man?

CLOWN
Good Sir Toby!
Good, Sir Toby.

OLIVIA
Cousin, cousin, how have you come so early by this
lethargy?
Now, cousin, why the lethargy this early?

SIR TOBY BELCH
Lechery! I defy lechery. There's one at the gate.   *115*
Lechery? I'm not lecherous. Someone's here.

OLIVIA
Ay, marry, what is he?
I know. Who is it?

SIR TOBY BELCH
Let him be the devil, an he will, I care not:
The devil, if he likes, for all I care.

give me faith, say I. Well, it's all one.
God's looking after me. Well, there you go.

[EXIT]

OLIVIA
What's a drunken man like, fool?
What is a drunken man like, fool?

CLOWN
Like a drowned man, a fool and a mad man: *120*
He's like a drowned man, and a fool, and mad.

one draught above heat makes him a fool;
One drink too many, he becomes a fool;

31

the second mads him; and a third drowns him.
the second turns him mad; the third, he drowns.

OLIVIA
Go thou and seek the crowner, and let him sit o' my
Go find the coroner; have him preside

coz; for he's in the third degree of drink,
over my cousin, for he's third-stage drunk,

he's drowned: go, look after him.   125
and, therefore, drowning. Go look after him.

CLOWN
He is but mad yet, madonna;
He's only at the mad stage now, madonna;

and the fool shall look to the madman.
but I will go and take good care of him.

[EXIT]

[RE-ENTER MALVOLIO]

MALVOLIO
Madam, yond young fellow swears he will speak with you.
Madam, that young man's adamant he'll speak to you.

I told him you were sick; he takes on him to
I told him you were sick; he said he knew that,

understand so much, and therefore comes to speak   130
and that's the reason why he's come to speak

with you. I told him you were asleep; he seems to
with you. I told him that you were asleep;

have a foreknowledge of that too, and therefore
he knew that too, and that's the reason why

comes to speak with you. What is to be said to him,
he's here to speak to you. What should I say,

lady? He's fortified against any denial.
my lady? He's determined to rebut excuses.

OLIVIA
Tell him he shall not speak with me.   135
Go tell him that he cannot speak with me.

MALVOLIO
Has been told so; and he says, he'll stand at your
I've told him that, and he said that he'd wait

door like a sheriff's post, and be the supporter to
outside your doorway like a lamppost, leaning

a bench, but he'll speak with you.
upon a bench until he speaks to you.

OLIVIA
What kind o' man is he?
What kind of man is he?

MALVOLIO
Why, of mankind.   140
Well...he's just like a man.

OLIVIA
What manner of man?
What type of man?

MALVOLIO
Of very ill manner; he'll speak with you, will you or no.
He's very rude. He'll speak, like it or not.

OLIVIA
Of what personage and years is he?
What does he look like, and how old is he?

MALVOLIO
Not yet old enough for a man, nor young enough for
Not old enough to be a man, nor young

a boy; as a squash is before 'tis a peascod, or a   145
enough to be a boy; he's like a pea seed

cooling when 'tis almost an apple: 'tis with him
before it is a pod; a pip, no apple.

in standing water, between boy and man. He is very
He's like the turning tide, not man nor boy.

well-favoured and he speaks very shrewishly;
He's handsome, with an oddly high-pitched voice.

one would think his mother's milk were scarce out of him.
You'd think he's just weaned off his mother's milk.

OLIVIA
Let him approach: call in my gentlewoman.   *150*
Let him come in. Go get my gentlewoman.

MALVOLIO
Gentlewoman, my lady calls.
Oh, gentlewoman, come; my lady wants you.

[EXIT]

[RE-ENTER MARIA]

OLIVIA
Give me my veil: come, throw it o'er my face.
Give me my veil and cover up my face.

We'll once more hear Orsino's embassy.
Let's hear Orsino's begging pleas again.

[ENTER VIOLA, AND ATTENDANTS]

VIOLA
The honourable lady of the house, which is she?
Which of you is the lady of the house?

OLIVIA
Speak to me; I shall answer for her.   *155*
Speak to me. I'll answer for her.

Your will?
What do you want?

VIOLA
Most radiant, exquisite and unmatchable beauty,--I
Most radiant, exquisite, unmatched beauty,

pray you, tell me if this be the lady of the house,
please state if you're the lady of the house,

for I never saw her: I would be loath to cast away
for I have not seen her before. I'd hate

my speech, for besides that it is excellently well penned,   *160*
to waste my speech, for, though it's been well written,

I have taken great pains to con it.
I've gone to great lengths just to memorise it.

Good beauties, let me sustain no scorn;
You lovely ladies, don't make fun of me;

I am very comptible, even to the least sinister usage.
I'm over-sensitive to criticism.

OLIVIA
Whence came you, sir?
Where are you from, sir?

VIOLA
I can say little more than I have studied, and that   165
I can't say more than I have memorised;

question's out of my part. Good gentle one,
I didn't learn that part. Good gentle lady,

give me modest assurance if you be the lady
give me some reassurance you're the lady

of the house, that I may proceed in my speech.
of this house, and then I'll begin my speech.

OLIVIA
Are you a comedian?
Are you an actor?

VIOLA
No, my profound heart: and yet, by the very fangs   170
Oh goodness, no! But I must reassure you

of malice I swear, I am not that I play.
my speech's words are not coming from me.

Are you the lady of the house?
Are you the lady of the house?

OLIVIA
If I do not usurp myself, I am.
If I don't overthrow myself, I am.

VIOLA
Most certain, if you are she, you do usurp
Indeed, if you are her, you overthrow

yourself; for what is yours to bestow is not yours   175
yourself; for all the love you have to give

to reserve. But this is from my commission:
can't be reserved by you. But I digress.

I will on with my speech in your praise,
I'll get on with my speech that praises you

35

and then show you the heart of my message.
and demonstrates the essence of my message.

OLIVIA
Come to what is important in't: I forgive you the praise.
Cut to the bits that matter; drop the praise.

VIOLA
Alas, I took great pains to study it, and 'tis poetical.   180
I'm sorry, but I learned it; it's poetic.

OLIVIA
It is the more like to be feigned: I pray you,
Then it's more likely insincere. I ask you

keep it in. I heard you were saucy at my gates,
drop the praise. I heard that you were rude

and allowed your approach rather to wonder at you
outside; I let you in because I'm curious

than to hear you. If you be not mad,
to see you, not to hear you. If you're sane,

be gone; if you have reason, be brief: 'tis not that time of   185
clear off; else, keep it brief. Now's not the time

moon with me to make one in so skipping a dialogue.
for me to listen to you waffling.

MARIA
Will you hoist sail, sir? Here lies your way.
Will you be setting sail, sir? Here's the exit.

VIOLA
No, good swabber; I am to hull here a little longer.
No, deck-hand, I'll moor here a little longer.

Some mollification for your giant, sweet lady.
Please pacify your giant maid, dear lady.

Tell me your mind: I am a messenger.   190
Speak on; tell me your thoughts. I'm just the messenger.

OLIVIA
Sure, you have some hideous matter to deliver, when
Surely you have an awful thing to say

the courtesy of it is so fearful. Speak your office.
because you have been god-awfully rude.

VIOLA
It alone concerns your ear. I bring no overture of
It's just for you to hear. I'm not declaring
war, no taxation of homage: I hold the olive in my
a war, or seeking tax. An olive branch
hand; my words are as fun of peace as matter.   *195*
I offer in my hand; I'm here in peace.

OLIVIA
Yet you began rudely. What are you? What would you?
But you were rude. Who are you? What do you want?

VIOLA
The rudeness that hath appeared in me have I
The rudeness that appeared in me I learnt
learned from my entertainment. What I am, and what I
from those who greeted me. Now what I am
would, are as secret as maidenhead;
and want are secret, like virginity.
to your ears, divinity, to any other's, profanation.   *200*
For your ears only; no one else can hear.

OLIVIA
Give us the place alone: we will hear this divinity.
Leave us alone. I'll listen to this secret.

[EXEUNT MARIA AND ATTENDANTS]

Now, sir, what is your text?
Now, sir, what is your message?

VIOLA
Most sweet lady,--
Most sweet lady—

OLIVIA
A comfortable doctrine, and much may be said of it.
A decent opening, quite comforting;
Where lies your text?   *205*
I'll give you that. Where is the message written?

VIOLA
In Orsino's bosom.
Upon Orsino's chest.

OLIVIA
In his bosom! In what chapter of his bosom?
Upon his chest? Where on his chest is it?

VIOLA
To answer by the method, in the first of his heart.
To tell the truth, it lies within his heart.

OLIVIA
O, I have read it: it is heresy. Have you no more to say?
I've read that, and I don't believe it. What else?

VIOLA
Good madam, let me see your face.   210
Good madam, let me see your face.

OLIVIA
Have you any commission from your lord to negotiate
Have you permission from your lord to speak

with my face? You are now out of your text:
directly to my face? You're now off script.

but we will draw the curtain and show you the picture.
But I'll lift up my veil and show my face.

Look you, sir, such a one I was this present:
Look, here's a portrait how I look today.

is't not well done?   215
It's rather nice, right?

[UNVEILING.]

VIOLA
Excellently done, if God did all.
It's beautiful, if that's how God intended.

OLIVIA
'Tis in grain, sir; 'twill endure wind and weather.
It's as I am, and won't change with the weather.

VIOLA
'Tis beauty truly blent, whose red and white
It is a blended beauty, red and white,

Nature's own sweet and cunning hand laid on:
Made by the sweet and cunning hand of nature.

Lady, you are the cruell'st she alive,   *220*
 Lady, you are the cruellest person living

If you will lead these graces to the grave
 If you will take your beauty to the grave

And leave the world no copy.
 Without leaving a child here of your own.

OLIVIA
O, sir, I will not be so hard-hearted; I will give
 Oh, sir, I'd never be so cruel! I'll list

out divers schedules of my beauty: it shall be
 each element of beauty, to include

inventoried, and every particle and utensil   *225*
 each part and particle of me, all listed

labelled to my will: as, item, two lips,
 and labelled as I want: an item—lips,

indifferent red; item, two grey eyes, with lids to them;
 reddish; an item—two grey eyes, with lids;

item, one neck, one chin, and so forth. Were
 an item– neck; a chin; and so forth. Were

you sent hither to praise me?
 you sent to praise me here?

VIOLA
I see you what you are, you are too proud;   *230*
 I see you as you are, and you're too proud.

But, if you were the devil, you are fair.
 But gorgeous, even if you were the devil.

My lord and master loves you: O, such love
 My lord and master loves you, and such love

Could be but recompensed, though you were crowned
 Should be rewarded even if you were

The nonpareil of beauty!
 Unequalled in your beauty.

OLIVIA
      How does he love me?   *235*
      How does he love me?

VIOLA
With adorations, fertile tears,
With words of deep affection, and with tears,

With groans that thunder love, with sighs of fire.
Combined with thunderous groans of tender love.

OLIVIA
Your lord does know my mind; I cannot love him:
Your lord knows my opinion. I can't love him.

Yet I suppose him virtuous, know him noble,
Although I guess he's nice, and know he's rich,

Of great estate, of fresh and stainless youth;   240
With lots of land, and innocently young;

In voices well divulged, free, learned and valiant;
Folk say he's kind and clever, and he's brave,

And in dimension and the shape of nature
And by the way he stands and of his posture,

A gracious person: but yet I cannot love him;
They say he's gracious. But I cannot love him.

He might have took his answer long ago.
He should have got the message long ago.

VIOLA
If I did love you in my master's flame,   245
If I loved you with all my master's passion,

With such a suffering, such a deadly life,
With so much suffering, like death in life,

In your denial I would find no sense;
Rejecting me would not make any sense.

I would not understand it.
I would not understand it.

OLIVIA
                       Why, what would you?
                      What would you do?

VIOLA
Make me a willow cabin at your gate,   250
I'd make a wooden cabin at your gate

And call upon my soul within the house;
And there I'd pray that you would want my soul;

40

Write loyal cantons of contemned love
I'd write you songs of love between two people
And sing them loud even in the dead of night;
And sing them loud into the dead of night,
Halloo your name to the reverberate hills
Praising your name to echo through the hills
And make the babbling gossip of the air   255
And make the blowing air whisper your name,
Cry out 'Olivia!' O, you should not rest
Shouting, "Olivia!" You could not rest
Between the elements of air and earth,
Alone on earth beneath a cloudy sky;
But you should pity me!
You'd sympathise with me.

OLIVIA
                You might do much.
                You'd do a lot.
What is your parentage?   260
What is your family's status?

VIOLA
Above my fortunes, yet my state is well:
Superior to now, but I'm OK.
I am a gentleman.
I am a gentleman.

OLIVIA
                Get you to your lord;
                Go back to your lord.
I cannot love him: let him send no more;
I cannot love him. Tell him, no more couriers...
Unless, perchance, you come to me again,   265
Unless, perhaps, you come to me again
To tell me how he takes it. Fare you well:
To tell me how he took the news. Goodbye.
I thank you for your pains: spend this for me.
And thank you for your troubles. Here's some money.

VIOLA

I am no fee'd post, lady; keep your purse:
There's no fee for this letter. Keep your money.

My master, not myself, lacks recompense.
My master, not myself, needs compensating.

Love make his heart of flint that you shall love;　　　　270
May Cupid make you love a heart of stone,

And let your fervour, like my master's, be
And may your love, just like my master's, be

Placed in contempt! Farewell, fair cruelty.
Rejected in contempt. Goodbye, cruel lady.

[EXIT]

OLIVIA

'What is your parentage?'
"What is your family's status?"

'Above my fortunes, yet my state is well:
"Superior to now, but I'm OK.

I am a gentleman.' I'll be sworn thou art;　　　　275
I am a gentleman." I'm sure you are.

Thy tongue, thy face, thy limbs, actions and spirit,
Your tongue, your face, your limbs, actions and spirit:

Do give thee five-fold blazon: not too fast:
Five proof-points you're a gentleman. Hang on!

soft, soft!
Wait a moment!

Unless the master were the man. How now!
What if Orsino was like him—then what?

Even so quickly may one catch the plague?　　　　280
Can someone really fall in love that fast?

Methinks I feel this youth's perfections
I feel like those perfections of that youth

With an invisible and subtle stealth
Are subtly, invisibly invading

To creep in at mine eyes. Well, let it be.
Into my eyes and mind. Well, let it be.

What ho, Malvolio!
Hello, Malvolio!

[RE-ENTER MALVOLIO]

MALVOLIO
Here, madam, at your service.   285
Hello madam, I'm back and at your service.

OLIVIA
Run after that same peevish messenger,
Go after that ill-natured messenger,

The county's man: he left this ring behind him,
Orsino's man. He left this ring behind,

Would I or not: tell him I'll none of it.
Regardless if I wanted it. I don't.

Desire him not to flatter with his lord,
Tell him he mustn't overpraise his lord,

Nor hold him up with hopes; I am not for him: 290
Nor give him any hope. He's not for me.

If that the youth will come this way to-morrow,
But if that youth comes back this way tomorrow,

I'll give him reasons for't: hie thee, Malvolio.
I'll tell him why. Quickly, Malvolio.

MALVOLIO
Madam, I will.
Madam, I will.

[EXIT]

OLIVIA
I do I know not what, and fear to find
I don't know what I'm doing, but I fear

Mine eye too great a flatterer for my mind.   295
My mind's usurped by what my eyes revere.

Fate, show thy force: ourselves we do not owe;
Fate, show your strength! You choose my destiny,

What is decreed must be, and be this so.
And what you choose for me to be will be.

[EXIT]

ACT 2

ACT 2, SCENE 1

THE SEA-COAST.

[ENTER ANTONIO AND SEBASTIAN]

ANTONIO
Will you stay no longer? Nor will you not that I go with you?
Won't you stay longer? Don't you want me with you?

SEBASTIAN
By your patience, no. My stars shine darkly over
If you don't mind, then no, for Lady Luck's

me: the malignancy of my fate might perhaps
unkind to me right now. I'd hate my luck

distemper yours; therefore I shall crave of you your
to rub off on you. And, therefore, I beg

leave that I may bear my evils alone: it were a bad   5
you take your leave and I'll suffer alone.

recompense for your love, to lay any of them on you.
How awful to repay you with misfortune!

ANTONIO
Let me yet know of you whither you are bound.
You can at least advise me where you're going.

SEBASTIAN
No, sooth, sir: my determinate voyage is mere
Well, no, I can't, for I'm just wandering

extravagancy. But I perceive in you so excellent a
without a place in mind. But I can see

touch of modesty, that you will not extort from me   10
that you are courteous and won't demand

what I am willing to keep in; therefore it charges
I tell you things I'd rather not. And so,

me in manners the rather to express myself.
with courtesy, I'll clarify my points.

47

You must know of me then, Antonio, my name is Sebastian,
You must have heard of me: I am Sebastian,

which I called Roderigo. My father was that
nickname Roderigo; and my father was

Sebastian of Messaline, whom I know you have heard of.   *15*
Sebastian of Messaline, who you've heard of.

He left behind him myself and a sister,
Now, when he died, he left me and my sister,

both born in an hour: if the heavens had been pleased,
both born an hour apart. How now I wish

would we had so ended! But you, sir, altered that;
we'd died so close! But you, sir, stopped that,

for some hour before you took me from the breach of
because, within an hour from saving me

the sea was my sister drowned.   *20*
out of the breaking waves, my sister drowned.

ANTONIO
Alas the day!
That was a tragic day!

SEBASTIAN
A lady, sir, though it was said she much resembled
Although a lady, many said she looked

me, was yet of many accounted beautiful: but,
like me; they called her beautiful; although

though I could not with such estimable wonder
I find it humbly difficult to think

overfar believe that, yet thus far I will boldly   *25*
too much of that, I will confess I bragged

publish her; she bore a mind that envy could not but
about her; those that envied her admit

call fair. She is drowned already, sir, with salt water,
her mind was kind. She drowned in salty water,

though I seem to drown her remembrance again with more.
And now my salty tears remind me of her.

ANTONIO
Pardon me, sir, your bad entertainment.
Forgive my awful hospitality.

SEBASTIAN

O good Antonio, forgive me your trouble.   30

My dear Antonio, forgive my troubles.

ANTONIO

If you will not murder me for my love,

If, for my love, you will not murder me,

let me be your servant.

then let me be your servant.

SEBASTIAN

If you will not undo what you have done,

If you will not undo your saving of me—

that is, kill him whom you have recovered, desire it not.

that is, you'll kill the one you rescued—then don't ask me.

Fare ye well at once: my bosom is full of kindness,   35

Goodbye. My heart is full of gratitude

and I am yet so near the manners of my mother, that

and I'm so like my mother, that just like her

upon the least occasion more mine eyes will tell

in circumstances like this, my eyes reveal

tales of me. I am bound to the Count Orsino's court: farewell.

the truth. I'm off to Count Orsino's court. Goodbye.

[EXIT]

ANTONIO

The gentleness of all the gods go with thee!

The gentleness of all the gods go with you!

I have many enemies in Orsino's court,   40

I've enemies in Count Orsino's court;

Else would I very shortly see thee there.

If not, I'd see you there again quite soon.

But, come what may, I do adore thee so,

But, whatever the outcome, I adore you,

That danger shall seem sport, and I will go.

And though there's danger, I will go there for you.

[EXIT]

ACT 2, SCENE 2

A STREET.

[ENTER VIOLA, MALVOLIO FOLLOWING]

MALVOLIO
Were not you even now with the Countess Olivia?
Weren't you just with Countess Olivia?

VIOLA
Even now, sir; on a moderate pace I have since
I was just now, sir. But, at moderate pace,
arrived but hither.
I've only got this far.

MALVOLIO
She returns this ring to you, sir: you might have
She wants to give this ring back, sir. You might
saved me my pains, to have taken it away yourself.   5
have saved me all the effort leaving with it.
She adds, moreover, that you should put your lord
She adds, as well, that you should tell your lord
into a desperate assurance she will none of him:
in no uncertain terms, she won't be with him.
and one thing more, that you be never so hardy to
And one more thing: don't be so bold to come
come again in his affairs, unless it be to report
back here again, unless it is to tell
your lord's taking of this. Receive it so.   10
of how your lord received this. Take it back.

VIOLA
She took the ring of me: I'll none of it.
She took the ring from me. I will not take it.

50

MALVOLIO

Come, sir, you peevishly threw it to her;
You threw it at her out of irritation,

and her will is, it should be so returned: if it be worth
and now she wants to throw it back. If it's worth

stooping for, there it lies in your eye; if not, be
bending for, there it is. If not, well then

it his that finds it.   15
it's his who finds it.

[EXIT]

VIOLA

I left no ring with her: what means this lady?
I left no ring with her. What does she mean?

Fortune forbid my outside have not charmed her!
Oh, don't say my appearance might have charmed her!

She made good view of me; indeed, so much,
She did look at me closely, so much so

That sure methought her eyes had lost her tongue,
I thought at times that she was lost for words,

For she did speak in starts distractedly.   20
And when she spoke, she spoke in fits and starts.

She loves me, sure; the cunning of her passion
She definitely loves me! Out of passion,

Invites me in this churlish messenger.
She showed me through her surly messenger.

None of my lord's ring! Why, he sent her none.
She won't take my lord's rings? He sent her none!

I am the man: if it be so, as 'tis,
I am the man she loves! If so, as is,

Poor lady, she were better love a dream.   25
She would be better off loving a dream.

Disguise, I see, thou art a wickedness,
I see that my disguise can be so evil,

Wherein the pregnant enemy does much.
It lets the devil do god-awful things.

How easy is it for the proper-false
How easy is it for deceptive men

In women's waxen hearts to set their forms!
To stamp their mark on women's hearts, like wax!

Alas, our frailty is the cause, not we!　　　　　　　　*30*
Regrettably, our weakness is the reason,

For such as we are made of, such we be.
And for this weakness, we create our treason.

How will this fadge? My master loves her dearly;
What will occur? My master loves her dearly,

And I, poor monster, fond as much on him;
And I, both man and woman, dote on him,

And she, mistaken, seems to dote on me.
And she, mistaken, seems to dote on me.

What will become of this? As I am man,　　　　　　　*35*
Oh, what on earth will happen? As a man,

My state is desperate for my master's love;
I have no hope of my own master's love.

As I am woman,--now alas the day!--
And as a woman—now, I rue the day!—

What thriftless sighs shall poor Olivia breathe!
Olivia's words of love will all be wasted.

O time! Thou must untangle this, not I;
Oh time, you must untangle this, not I.

It is too hard a knot for me to untie!　　　　　　　*40*
This knot's too tight for me to now untie!

[EXIT]

ACT 2, SCENE 3

OLIVIA'S HOUSE.

[ENTER SIR TOBY BELCH AND SIR ANDREW]

SIR TOBY BELCH
Approach, Sir Andrew: not to be abed after
Come over here, Sir Andrew. Staying up

midnight is to be up betimes; and 'diluculo
past midnight means we're both up early; doctors

surgere', thou know'st,--
say that's a good thing.

SIR ANDREW
Nay, my troth, I know not: but I know, to be up
I'm not so sure. But I am sure to be up

late is to be up late.   5
late means we are both up late.

SIR TOBY BELCH
A false conclusion: I hate it as an unfilled can.
A wrong conclusion, worse than empty tankards.

To be up after midnight and to go to bed then, is
To go to bed past midnight means that it's

early: so that to go to bed after midnight is to go
still early, and so bed past midnight means

to bed betimes. Does not our life consist of the
an early night. Aren't we just made up of

four elements?   10
the basic elements?

SIR ANDREW
Faith, so they say; but I think it rather consists
Well, so they say, but I believe we're made up

of eating and drinking.
of food and booze.

SIR TOBY BELCH
Thou'rt a scholar; let us therefore eat and drink.
Wise words, indeed. So let's both eat and drink.

Marian, I say! A stoup of wine!
Hey Marian, bring us a jug of wine!

[ENTER CLOWN]

SIR ANDREW
Here comes the fool, i' faith.   15
Eh up, here comes the fool.

CLOWN
How now, my hearts! Did you never see the picture
Hello, my petals! Have you seen the painting,

of 'we three'?
"We Three" with two asses, and you're the third?

SIR TOBY BELCH
Welcome, ass. Now let's have a catch.
Oh welcome, ass! Now, let's all have a chat.

SIR ANDREW
By my troth, the fool has an excellent breast.
This fool has got a lovely singing voice.

I had rather than forty shillings I had such a leg,   20
I'd give two pounds to dance as well as him,

and so sweet a breath to sing, as the fool has.
and sing as sweetly as that fool can sing.

In sooth, thou wast in very gracious fooling last
In truth, you were particularly funny

night, when thou spokest of Pigrogromitus, of the
last night when talking gibberish about

Vapians passing the equinoctial of Queubus:
made-up astronomy of random stars.

'twas very good, i' faith. I sent thee sixpence for thy   25
Well done. I tipped you with a coin to give to

leman: hadst it?
your sweetheart. You got it?

CLOWN
I did impeticos thy gratillity; for Malvolio's nose
I spent it, so Malvolio the nosey

is no whipstock: my lady has a white hand, and the
can keep his nose out; my lady's taste's refined:

Myrmidons are no bottle-ale houses.
she won't drink beer out of the bottle.

SIR ANDREW
Excellent! Why, this is the best fooling, when all is done.   30
How excellent! This is the finest humour.

Now, a song.
It's time now for a song!

SIR TOBY BELCH
Come on; there is sixpence for you: let's have a song.
Come on, here's sixpence. Give us all a song.

SIR ANDREW
There's a testril of me too: if one knight give a--
And here's the same from me. If one knight gave a...

CLOWN
Would you have a love-song, or a song of good life?
A love song or a song about good life?

SIR TOBY BELCH
A love-song, a love-song.   35
A love song, a love song.

SIR ANDREW
Ay, ay: I care not for good life.
Oh yes, I do not care about a good life.

CLOWN
[Sings]
O mistress mine, where are you roaming?
My lover, dear, where are you roaming?

O, stay and hear; your true love's coming,
Oh listen here! Your truelove's coming,

That can sing both high and low:
That can sing both high and low,

Trip no further, pretty sweeting;   40
Don't dance away, my little sweeting,

Journeys end in lovers meeting,
Journeys end in lovers meeting,

Every wise man's son doth know.
Every wise man's son does know.

SIR ANDREW
Excellent good, i' faith.
Excellent, I tell you.

SIR TOBY BELCH
Good, good.
Good, good.

CLOWN
[Sings]
What is love? 'Tis not hereafter;   45
What is love? It's not tomorrow.

Present mirth hath present laughter;
Humour now makes laughter follow.

What's to come is still unsure:
What's to come is still unclear.

In delay there lies no plenty;
There is no point in wasting time

Then come kiss me, sweet and twenty,
So kiss me now whilst in your prime.

Youth's a stuff will not endure.   50
We don't stay young for every year.

SIR ANDREW
A mellifluous voice, as I am true knight.
A pleasing, lovely voice, as I'm a knight.

SIR TOBY BELCH
A contagious breath.
Infectious vocals.

SIR ANDREW
Very sweet and contagious, i' faith.
Both very sweet and catchy, I believe.

SIR TOBY BELCH
To hear by the nose, it is dulcet in contagion.
If listening through the nose, it would smell sweet.

But shall we make the welkin dance indeed? 55
But shall we make the heavens dance, indeed?

Shall we rouse the night-owl in a catch that will
And maybe wake the creatures of the night,

draw three souls out of one weaver? Shall we do that?
and shake three souls out of a pious weaver?

SIR ANDREW
An you love me, let's do't: I am dog at a catch.
Oh yes, let's dance. I'm like a dog on heat.

CLOWN
By'r lady, sir, and some dogs will catch well.
Oh yes, come on, let's do the dancing dog.

SIR ANDREW
Most certain. Let our catch be, 'Thou knave.' 60
Oh, good! Let's sing the tune we know, "Our Knave."

CLOWN
'Hold thy peace, thou knave', knight?
The one that goes, "be quiet, fool", you mean?

I shall be constrained in't to call thee knave, knight.
If so, then I'm obliged to call you foolish.

SIR ANDREW
'Tis not the first time I have constrained one to
It's not the first time I've behaved for one

call me knave. Begin, fool: it begins 'Hold thy peace.'
to call me foolish. Start with "Hold thy peace."

CLOWN
I shall never begin if I hold my peace. 65
I won't get started if I hold my 'piece'.

SIR ANDREW
Good, i' faith. Come, begin.
Ha ha, touché. Come on, let's sing.

[CATCH SUNG]

[ENTER MARIA]

MARIA
What a caterwauling do you keep here! If my lady
What screeching cats are you folk keeping here?

have not called up her steward Malvolio and bid him
Call me a liar, but my lady ordered

turn you out of doors, never trust me.
Malvolio to throw you out the doors.

SIR TOBY BELCH
My lady's a Cataian, we are politicians, Malvolio's   70
My lady's bluffing; we're too smart; Malvolio's

a Peg-a-Ramsey, and 'Three merry men be we.'
a busy-body. "We're three merry men."

Am not I consanguineous? Am I not of her blood?
Aren't I related? Aren't we family?

Tillyvally. Lady!
So, do one, lady!

[Sings]
'There dwelt a man in Babylon, lady, lady!'
"There was once a man who lived in Babylon, dear lady."

CLOWN
Beshrew me, the knight's in admirable fooling.   75
This knight's in splendid mocking form tonight.

SIR ANDREW
Ay, he does well enough if he be disposed,
Oh yes, he does it well when he gets going,

and so do I too: he does it with a better grace,
and so do I. He's ruder than me at it,

but I do it more natural.
but I'm more of a natural.

SIR TOBY BELCH
[Sings]
'O, the twelfth day of December,'--
"On the twelfth day of December..."

MARIA
For the love o' God, peace!   80
Oh, for the love of God, shut up!

[ENTER MALVOLIO]

58

MALVOLIO

My masters, are you mad? Or what are you? Have ye
Good lord, are you all mad? What's this? Don't you have

no wit, manners, nor honesty, but to gabble like
manners or decency to not all bellow

tinkers at this time of night? Do ye make an
like drunkards late at night? Do you propose

alehouse of my lady's house, that ye squeak out your
to make my lady's house a pub, where you shout

coziers' catches without any mitigation or remorse   85
your cobbler's songs without concern about

of voice? Is there no respect of place, persons, nor
the noise? Don't you respect this place, the people,

time in you?
or even what the time is?

SIR TOBY BELCH

We did keep time, sir, in our catches. Sneck up!
We do keep time, sir, in our singing. Clear off!

MALVOLIO

Sir Toby, I must be round with you. My lady bade me
Sir Toby, I'll be blunt. My lady told me

tell you, that, though she harbours you as her   90
to tell you, though she puts you up because

kinsman, she's nothing allied to your disorders.
you are a relative, she hates your conduct.

If you can separate yourself and your misdemeanours,
If you can split yourself from your behaviour,

you are welcome to the house; if not, an it would please
you're welcome in this house; but if you can't,

you to take leave of her, she is very willing to bid
it's better that you leave; she's very willing

you farewell.   95
to say goodbye to you.

SIR TOBY BELCH

'Farewell, dear heart, since I must needs be gone.'
"Goodbye, my dear, it's time that I was gone."

59

MARIA
Nay, good Sir Toby.
No, good Sir Toby.

CLOWN
'His eyes do show his days are almost done.'
"His eyes look like his days are nearly done."

MALVOLIO
Is't even so?
So it's like this, then?

SIR TOBY BELCH
'But I will never die.'   100
"But I will never die."

CLOWN
Sir Toby, there you lie.
"Sir Toby, there you lie."

MALVOLIO
This is much credit to you.
Congratulations on this fine behaviour.

SIR TOBY BELCH
'Shall I bid him go?'
"Shall I ask him to leave?"

CLOWN
'What an if you do?'
"But what would that achieve?"

SIR TOBY BELCH
'Shall I bid him go, and spare not?'   105
"Shall I tell him to leave without a care?"

CLOWN
'O no, no, no, no, you dare not.'
"Oh no, no, no, no, no; you wouldn't dare."

SIR TOBY BELCH
Out o' tune, sir: ye lie. Art any more than a
You out of songs? I doubt it. Are you more
steward? Dost thou think, because thou art
than just a servant? And, as you are good,

60

virtuous, there shall be no more cakes and ale?
do you believe all others can't have fun?

CLOWN
Yes, by Saint Anne, and ginger shall be hot i' the 110
He does, by mother-of-Mary, and he won't let
mouth too.
ginger spice it up.

SIR TOBY BELCH
Thou'rt i' the right. Go, sir, rub your chain with
You're right, you know. Go polish up your necklace with
crumbs. A stoup of wine, Maria!
some breadcrumbs. Now, a jug of wine, Maria!

MALVOLIO
Mistress Mary, if you prized my lady's favour at any
Now, Mary, if you value the opinion
thing more than contempt, you would not give means 115
of my lady in the slightest, don't give
for this uncivil rule: she shall know of it, by this hand.
support to this unruly lot. I'll tell her!

[EXIT]

MARIA
Go shake your ears.
Go shake your ears, you silly ass!

SIR ANDREW
'Twere as good a deed as to drink when a man's
It's just about as useful drinking water
a-hungry, to challenge him the field, and then to
when hungry as when challenging to fight
break promise with him and make a fool of him. 120
and then not showing up to make him look a fool.

SIR TOBY BELCH
Do't, knight: I'll write thee a challenge: or I'll
Do it then, knight; I'll write the challenge for you,
deliver thy indignation to him by word of mouth.
and tell him of your outrage to his face.

MARIA
Sweet Sir Toby, be patient for tonight: since the
Dear Sir Toby, enough tonight, because
youth of the count's was today with thy lady, she is
the Count's young boy was here today, and she's had
much out of quiet. For Monsieur Malvolio, let me   125
no peace. And leave me with Malvolio
alone with him: if I do not gull him into a
alone. If I can't trick him into being
nayword, and make him a common recreation, do not
an ass, and make him look a fool, then I'm
think I have wit enough to lie straight in my bed:
not smart enough to lay straight in my bed.
I know I can do it.
I know that I can do it.

SIR TOBY BELCH
Possess us, possess us; tell us something of him.   130
Oh tell us, tell us something of your plan!

MARIA
Marry, sir, sometimes he is a kind of puritan.
Sometimes he's strict and morally conformist.

SIR ANDREW
O, if I thought that I'ld beat him like a dog!
If I'd have known, I'd beat him like a dog!

SIR TOBY BELCH
What, for being a puritan? Thy exquisite reason,
For being moral? Is that really fair,
dear knight?
dear knight?

SIR ANDREW
I have no exquisite reason for't, but I have reason   135
Perhaps it is not fair, but for me,
good enough.
it's reason nonetheless.

MARIA
The devil a puritan that he is, or any thing
He is about as moral as the devil,

62

constantly, but a time-pleaser; an affected ass,
and says just what you want to hear; that dumb ass

that cons state without book and utters it by great
learns worthy words by heart, then just repeats them;

swarths: the best persuaded of himself,   *140*
he holds such high opinion of himself

so crammed, as he thinks, with excellencies, that it is
that, due to all his splendid qualities,

his grounds of faith that all that look on him love
he thinks that all who see him think he's great.

him; and on that vice in him will my revenge find
And, with this vanity of his, I'll find

notable cause to work.
a way to get revenge.

SIR TOBY BELCH
What wilt thou do?   *145*
What will you do?

MARIA
I will drop in his way some obscure epistles of love;
I'll make him find some vague letters of love,

wherein, by the colour of his beard, the shape
which—by the way they crave his coloured beard,

of his leg, the manner of his gait, the expressure
his leg shape and the way he walks, his eyes,

of his eye, forehead, and complexion, he shall find
his forehead, and complexion—he'll believe

himself most feelingly personated. I can write very   *150*
they are describing him. I write just like

like my lady your niece: on a forgotten matter we
my lady, who's your niece; I had forgotten,

can hardly make distinction of our hands.
there's hardly a distinction in our writing.

SIR TOBY BELCH
Excellent! I smell a device.
Quite excellent! I think I smell a plan.

SIR ANDREW
I have't in my nose too.
  I think I smell it, too.

SIR TOBY BELCH
He shall think, by the letters that thou wilt drop,   155
  He's going to think, through letters that you write,

that they come from my niece, and that she's in
  that they are from my niece, and that she is

love with him.
  in love with him.

MARIA
My purpose is, indeed, a horse of that colour.
  That is my purpose, like a horse is brown.

SIR ANDREW
And your horse now would make him an ass.
  And now your horse will make him look an ass!

MARIA
Ass, I doubt not.   160
  An ass, I do not doubt it.

SIR ANDREW
O, 'twill be admirable!
  It's going to be quite wonderful!

MARIA
Sport royal, I warrant you: I know my physic will
  A right old laugh, I tell you. And I'm sure

work with him. I will plant you two, and let the
  this plan will work. I'll get you two to hide—

fool make a third, where he shall find the letter:
  and with the fool makes three—where he will find

observe his construction of it. For this night, to bed,   165
  the letter. Watch him read it. Now, it's bedtime,

and dream on the event. Farewell.
  and I will dream about it there. Farewell.

[EXIT]

64

SIR TOBY BELCH
Good night, Penthesilea.
Good night, tough Amazonian warrior.

SIR ANDREW
Before me, she's a good wench.
I tell you, she's a proper cracking lass.

SIR TOBY BELCH
She's a beagle, true-bred, and one that adores me:
A thoroughbred, she is, and she adores me.

what o' that?   *170*
How could it be?

SIR ANDREW
I was adored once too.
I was adored once, too.

SIR TOBY BELCH
Let's to bed, knight. Thou hadst need send for
It's time for bed now, knight. You need to get

more money.
some money sent.

SIR ANDREW
If I cannot recover your niece, I am a foul way out.
If I can't pull your niece, I'm going broke.

SIR TOBY BELCH
Send for money, knight: if thou hast her not   *175*
Send for the money, knight. But if you don't

i' the end, call me cut.
bag her eventually, I'll be castrated!

SIR ANDREW
If I do not, never trust me, take it how you will.
And if I don't, I'll tell you not to trust me.

SIR TOBY BELCH
Come, come, I'll go burn some sack; 'tis too late
Come on, I'll make some mulled wine. It's too late

to go to bed now: come, knight; come, knight.
to go to bed now. Come on, knight; come on.

[EXEUNT]

ACT 2, SCENE 4

DUKE ORSINO'S PALACE.

[ENTER DUKE ORSINO, VIOLA, CURIO, AND OTHERS]

DUKE ORSINO
Give me some music. Now, good morrow, friends.
Play me some music. Now, good morning, friends.

Now, good Cesario, but that piece of song,
And now, Cesario, about that song

That old and antique song we heard last night:
We heard last night, that age-old rustic song;

Methought it did relieve my passion much,
I found that it relieved my aching heart

More than light airs and recollected terms   5
Much more than those repetitive plain tunes

Of these most brisk and giddy-paced times:
That seem to be the fashion of the times.

Come, but one verse.
Come on, just play a single verse for me.

CURIO
He is not here, so please your lordship that should sing it.
My lord, I'm sorry, but the singer's not here.

DUKE ORSINO
Who was it?
Who was it?

CURIO
Feste, the jester, my lord; a fool that the lady   10
That jester Feste, sir, the fool who made

Olivia's father took much delight in. He is about the house.
Lady Olivia's father laugh. He's somewhere here.

DUKE ORSINO
Seek him out, and play the tune the while.
Go find him; in the meantime, play the tune.

[EXIT CURIO. MUSIC PLAYS]

Come hither, boy: if ever thou shalt love,
Come over here, boy. If you find true love,

In the sweet pangs of it remember me;
In its enchanting anguish, think of me,

For such as I am all true lovers are,   15
For as I am now, all true lovers are,

Unstaid and skittish in all motions else,
Impulsive, unpredictable and skittish

Save in the constant image of the creature
At everything except the image of

That is beloved. How dost thou like this tune?
The one they truly love. D'you like this tune?

VIOLA
It gives a very echo to the seat
It gives a true reflection of the feeling

Where Love is throned.   20
Of perfect love.

DUKE ORSINO
                        Thou dost speak masterly:
                        You've called that perfectly.

My life upon't, young though thou art, thine eye
I bet my life, despite your age, your eyes

Hath stayed upon some favour that it loves:
Have spotted someone that you really love.

Hath it not, boy?
Is that not true?

VIOLA
                        A little, by your favour.   25
                        A bit, and thanks to you.

DUKE ORSINO
What kind of woman is't?
What type of woman, then?

VIOLA

Of your complexion.
Of your complexion.

DUKE ORSINO

She is not worth thee, then. What years, i' faith?
Then she's not good enough for you! How old?

VIOLA

About your years, my lord.
About as old as you, my lord.

DUKE ORSINO

Too old by heaven: let still the woman take   30
That's far too old, but women ought to marry

An elder than herself: so wears she to him,
An older man; she can adapt to him,

So sways she level in her husband's heart:
And then retain her husband's loving heart.

For, boy, however we do praise ourselves,
Because, although we brag about ourselves,

Our fancies are more giddy and unfirm,
Us men are frivolous with our affections;

More longing, wavering, sooner lost and worn,   35
We're overwhelmed with love that doesn't last,

Than women's are.
Unlike the love of women.

VIOLA

I think it well, my lord.
Yes, you're right.

DUKE ORSINO

Then let thy love be younger than thyself,
Then let the one you love be younger than you

Or thy affection cannot hold the bent;
Or your affection will not stay the course.

For women are as roses, whose fair flower   40
For women are like roses whose sweet flower

Being once displayed, doth fall that very hour.
They show just once; it's gone within the hour.

68

VIOLA
And so they are: alas, that they are so;
Ain't that the truth! How sad that is the way

To die, even when they to perfection grow!
That once they've bloomed, perfection doesn't stay.

[RE-ENTER CURIO AND CLOWN]

DUKE ORSINO
O, fellow, come, the song we had last night.
Good fellow, sing the song you sang last night.

Mark it, Cesario, it is old and plain;   45
Check this, Cesario. It's old and simple;

The spinsters and the knitters in the sun
The knitters spinning wool out in the sun

And the free maids that weave their thread with bones
And weavers using bobbins made of bone

Do use to chant it: it is silly sooth,
Sing it aloud. It tells the simple truth

And dallies with the innocence of love,
About the simple innocence of love

Like the old age.   50
In former times.

CLOWN
Are you ready, sir?
Are you ready, sir?

DUKE ORSINO
Ay; prithee, sing.
Yes. Please, sing.

[MUSIC]

CLOWN
[Sings song]
Come away, come away, death,
Take me now, take me now death,

And in sad cypress let me be laid;
In a coffin of cypress wood, lay me to sleep.

Fly away, fly away breath;   55
Go away, go away, breath,

69

I am slain by a fair cruel maid.
I died when that beautiful girl made me weep.

My shroud of white, stuck all with yew,
My white burial gown, with branches of yew,

O, prepare it!
Oh, prepare it!

My part of death, no one so true
Nobody so honest, with death—it is true—

Did share it.   60
Did share it.

Not a flower, not a flower sweet
Not a flower, not a flower sweet,

On my black coffin let there be strown;
Upon my black coffin let anyone throw,

Not a friend, not a friend greet
Not a friend, not a friend greet

My poor corpse, where my bones shall be thrown:
My poor corpse where my bones will all go.

A thousand thousand sighs to save,   65
This way a thousand sighs we'll save,

Lay me, O, where
So lay me where

Sad true lover never find my grave,
My sad true lover can't find my grave

To weep there!
to weep for me there.

DUKE ORSINO
There's for thy pains.
That's for your trouble.

CLOWN
No pains, sir: I take pleasure in singing, sir.   70
No trouble, sir. I take great pleasure singing.

DUKE ORSINO
I'll pay thy pleasure then.
I'll pay you for your pleasure, then.

CLOWN
Truly, sir, and pleasure will be paid, one time or another.
Really, no need. You'll pay it soon enough.

DUKE ORSINO
Give me now leave to leave thee.
Please leave me now to be alone.

CLOWN
Now, the melancholy god protect thee; and the
Now Saturn, God of sadness, please protect you,

tailor make thy doublet of changeable taffeta,   75
and may your tailor's jacket change its hue,

for thy mind is a very opal. I would have men
just like your mind, like opal. I'd have men

of such constancy put to sea, that their business might be
like that put out to sea so that their business

every thing and their intent every where; for that's
was all around them and they then could drift,

it that always makes a good voyage of nothing. Farewell.
for that's the way to make a trip from nothing. Goodbye.

[EXIT]

DUKE ORSINO
Let all the rest give place.   80
The rest of you can leave.

[CURIO AND ATTENDANTS RETIRE]

    Once more, Cesario,
    Once more, Cesario,

Get thee to yond same sovereign cruelty:
Go see my queen of hearts, Olivia,

Tell her, my love, more noble than the world,
And tell her that my love, the best there is,

Prizes not quantity of dirty lands;
Is not in need of winning any land.

The parts that fortune hath bestowed upon her,   85
The land, and things that she's inherited,

Tell her, I hold as giddily as fortune;
Tell her I have no interest in at all.

But 'tis that miracle and queen of gems
But it's that she's miraculously gorgeous,

That nature pranks her in attracts my soul.
Endowed with nature's gifts, that makes me want her.

VIOLA
But if she cannot love you, sir?
But if she cannot love you, sir?

DUKE ORSINO
I cannot be so answered.   90
That cannot be the answer.

VIOLA
                          Sooth, but you must.
                    But it must be.

Say that some lady, as perhaps there is,
Imagine that you're told about a lady

Hath for your love a great a pang of heart
Who has an equal, overwhelming love,

As you have for Olivia: you cannot love her;
As you have for Olivia. You can't love her;

You tell her so; must she not then be answered?   95
You tell her that. Shouldn't she just accept it?

DUKE ORSINO
There is no woman's sides
There is no woman able

Can bide the beating of so strong a passion
To tolerate the pain of so much passion

As love doth give my heart; no woman's heart
That beats within my heart; no woman's heart

So big, to hold so much; they lack retention
Can hold as much as mine; they can't retain it.

Alas, their love may be called appetite,   100
Regrettably, their love is more like hunger,

No motion of the liver, but the palate,
And not a deep emotion, but desire

That suffer surfeit, cloyment and revolt;
That can be overfed to make them sick.

But mine is all as hungry as the sea,
But my love is unbounding, like the ocean,

And can digest as much: make no compare
And can consume as much. Do not compare

Between that love a woman can bear me   *105*
The love a woman might declare for me

And that I owe Olivia.
As my love for Olivia.

VIOLA
Ay, but I know--
Yes, but I know...

DUKE ORSINO
What dost thou know?
What do you know?

VIOLA
Too well what love women to men may owe:
I know too well how women love their man.

In faith, they are as true of heart as we.   *110*
In truth, they love the same as you or I.

My father had a daughter loved a man,
My father's daughter loved a man, and maybe,

As it might be, perhaps, were I a woman,
If I'd have been a woman, then perhaps,

I should your lordship.
I might have loved you that much.

DUKE ORSINO
              And what's her history?
                  Then what happened?

VIOLA
A blank, my lord. She never told her love,   *115*
Then nothing happened, for she never told him,

But let concealment, like a worm i' the bud,
But hid it, like a worm hides in a rose bud

Feed on her damask cheek: she pined in thought,
And eats away at it. She pined for him

And with a green and yellow melancholy
With melancholic, love-sick jealously,

73

She sat like patience on a monument,
And endlessly sat on a monument,

Smiling at grief. Was not this love indeed?   120
Smiling in grief. So, is that not true love?

We men may say more, swear more: but indeed
Us men may talk, declaring our true love more,

Our shows are more than will; for still we prove
Yet, we're more talk than action, demonstrating

Much in our vows, but little in our love.
Few acts of love whilst we're off remonstrating.

DUKE ORSINO
But died thy sister of her love, my boy?
But did your sister die from love, my boy?

VIOLA
I am all the daughters of my father's house,   125
I'm every daughter that my father raised

And all the brothers too: and yet I know not.
And all the brothers too, but I can't answer.

Sir, shall I to this lady?
Shall I deliver this to her?

DUKE ORSINO
                                    Ay, that's the theme.
Yes, do.

To her in haste; give her this jewel; say,
And get there quick. Give her this jewel. Say

My love can give no place, bide no denay.   130
She can't resist; my love won't go away.

[EXEUNT]

ACT 2, SCENE 5

OLIVIA'S GARDEN.

[ENTER SIR TOBY BELCH, SIR ANDREW, AND FABIAN]

SIR TOBY BELCH
Come thy ways, Signior Fabian.
Come along, Signior Fabian.

FABIAN
Nay, I'll come: if I lose a scruple of this sport,
I'm coming! If I miss a moment's mockery

let me be boiled to death with melancholy.
then boil me to death with endless sadness.

SIR TOBY BELCH
Wouldst thou not be glad to have the niggardly
Won't you be glad to see that condescending,

rascally sheep-biter come by some notable shame?   5
back-stabbing goon downright humiliated?

FABIAN
I would exult, man: you know, he brought me out o'
I'd love it, mate. You know he got me in

favour with my lady about a bear-baiting here.
to trouble with my lady when bearbaiting.

SIR TOBY BELCH
To anger him we'll have the bear again; and we will
To wind him up, let's get the bear again,

fool him black and blue: shall we not, Sir Andrew?
and trick him into beating up himself, hey Sir Andrew?

SIR ANDREW
An we do not, it is pity of our lives.   10
If not, we will regret it all our lives.

SIR TOBY BELCH
Here comes the little villain.
Here comes the little rascal.

[ENTER MARIA]

How now, my metal of India!
What's occurring, my dearest girl of gold?

MARIA
Get ye all three into the box-tree: Malvolio's
You three, go hide behind the hedge. Malvolio
coming down this walk: he has been yonder i' the
is walking down the path. He's been outside
sun practising behaviour to his own shadow   15
to practise his behaviour to his shadow
this half hour: observe him, for the love of mockery;
for half an hour. Watch him for a laugh,
for I know this letter will make a contemplative idiot of him.
because that letter will make him a fool.
Close, in the name of jesting!
Hide, in the name of true tomfoolery!
Lie thou there,
I'll put this letter here,

[Throws down a letter]

for here comes the trout that must be caught with tickling. 20
because here comes the fish we'll catch through mockery.

[EXIT]

[ENTER MALVOLIO]

MALVOLIO
'Tis but fortune; all is fortune. Maria once told
It is just luck, sheer luck. Maria told me
me she did affect me: and I have heard herself come
that once she liked me; I have heard her say
thus near, that, should she fancy, it should be one
that if she fell in love, it would be with
of my complexion. Besides, she uses me with a more
someone who looks like me. And she thinks of me

exalted respect than any one else that follows her.
   with greater admiration than all others.

What should I think on't?
   So, then, what should I believe?

SIR TOBY BELCH
Here's an overweening rogue!
   He's such a pompous twerp.

FABIAN
O, peace! Contemplation makes a rare
   Oh, shush! His contemplation makes him more

turkey-cock of him: how he jets under his advanced plumes!
   a snooty peacock. Watch him preen his feathers!

SIR ANDREW
'Slight, I could so beat the rogue!   30
   Good gracious, how I'd like to punch this twit!

SIR TOBY BELCH
Peace, I say.
   Be quiet, I tell you.

MALVOLIO
To be Count Malvolio!
   Imagine this: I'm Count Malvolio.

SIR TOBY BELCH
Ah, rogue!
   You goon!

SIR ANDREW
Pistol him, pistol him.
   Shoot him, shoot him!

SIR TOBY BELCH
Peace, peace!   35
   Quiet!

MALVOLIO
There is example for't; the lady of the Strachy
   It has been done before: the lady from

married the yeoman of the wardrobe.
   the Strachy village wed her wardrobe-man.

SIR ANDREW
Fie on him, Jezebel!
God damn this man!

FABIAN
O, peace! Now he's deeply in: look how
Be quiet! For he's fallen for our trap,

imagination blows him.   40
and his imagination pumps his ego.

MALVOLIO
Having been three months married to her,
And three months after I've been wed to her,

sitting in my state,--
sat in my state room...

SIR TOBY BELCH
O, for a stone-bow, to hit him in the eye!
I wish I had a catapult to stone him!

MALVOLIO
Calling my officers about me, in my branched velvet gown;
...I'll convene my servants, in my embroidered gown,

having come from a day-bed, where I have left   45
returning from my daybed, having left

Olivia sleeping,--
Olivia sleeping...

SIR TOBY BELCH
Fire and brimstone!
All hell's breaking loose!

FABIAN
O, peace, peace!
Oh, shush, shush!

MALVOLIO
And then to have the humour of state; and after a
...and then adopt a high-and-mighty pose;

demure travel of regard, telling them I know my   50
and after I had gently scoured the room,

place as I would they should do theirs,
confirming my position and them theirs,

to for my kinsman Toby,--
I'd call upon my relative, Sir Toby...

SIR TOBY BELCH
Bolts and shackles!
Well, bloody hell!

FABIAN
O peace, peace, peace! Now, now.
Oh, peace, be quiet now!

MALVOLIO
Seven of my people, with an obedient start, make   55
Then seven servants leave obediently

out for him: I frown the while; and perchance wind
to find him. I will frown awhile, and maybe wind up

up watch, or play with my--some rich jewel. Toby
my watch, or fiddle with...some jewellery. Toby

approaches; courtesies there to me,--
comes, and bows before me...

SIR TOBY BELCH
Shall this fellow live?
Will this chap take our bait?

FABIAN
Though our silence be drawn from us with cars, yet peace. 60
He will if we keep quiet, so shut up!

MALVOLIO
I extend my hand to him thus, quenching my familiar
I'll hold my hand to him like this, resisting

smile with an austere regard of control,--
the urge to smile, a stern look of control...

SIR TOBY BELCH
And does not Toby take you a blow o' the lips then?
Then won't Sir Toby punch you in the face?

MALVOLIO
Saying, 'Cousin Toby, my fortunes having cast me on
...saying, "My cousin Toby, my good fortune

your niece give me this prerogative of speech,'--   65
in marrying your niece means I can say this..."

SIR TOBY BELCH
What, what?
  Say what?

MALVOLIO
'You must amend your drunkenness.'
  "You must stop getting drunk."

SIR TOBY BELCH
Out, scab!
  Sod off, twerp!

FABIAN
Nay, patience, or we break the sinews of our plot.
  No, wait, or we'll destroy the plot we have!

MALVOLIO
'Besides, you waste the treasure of your time with   70
  "Besides, you're wasting all your precious time

a foolish knight,'--
  with an idiotic knight..."

SIR ANDREW
That's me, I warrant you.
  That's me, I bet you!

MALVOLIO
'One Sir Andrew,'--
  "That Sir Andrew."

SIR ANDREW
I knew 'twas I; for many do call me fool.
  I knew he meant me! Many call me foolish.

MALVOLIO
What employment have we here?   75
  What business have we here?

[TAKING UP THE LETTER]

FABIAN
Now is the woodcock near the gin.
  The foolish bird is eyeing up our trap.

SIR TOBY BELCH
O, peace! And the spirit of humour intimate
  Hush, in the name of humour, let's all hope

reading aloud to him!
he reads it out aloud.

MALVOLIO
By my life, this is my lady's hand these be her
I bet my life this is my lady's writing!

very C's, her U's and her T's and thus makes she her   80
These letters are her c's, her u's and t's,

great P's. It is, in contempt of question, her hand.
and capital P's. It's definitely her handwriting.

SIR ANDREW
Her C's, her U's and her T's: why that?
Her c's, her u's, her t's. What letter's missing?

MALVOLIO
[Reads]
'To the unknown beloved, this, and my good
"To him who does not know I love him so,

wishes:'--her very phrases! By your leave, wax.
best wishes." They're her words! I'll break this wax seal;

Soft! And the impressure her Lucrece, with which she   85
this imprint in the wax is from the stamp

uses to seal: 'tis my lady. To whom should this be?
she seals her envelopes. It's her! Who's it addressed to?

FABIAN
This wins him, liver and all.
This will wholeheartedly convince him.

MALVOLIO
[Reads]
Jove knows I love: But who?
I am in love, by Jove, but who's the beau?

Lips, do not move;
Be still, my lips, don't move:

No man must know.   90
No man must know.

'No man must know.' What follows? The numbers
"No man must know." What's after that? The rhythm

altered! 'No man must know:' if this should be
has changed. "No man must know." This could be you,

81

thee, Malvolio?
Malvolio!

SIR TOBY BELCH
Marry, hang thee, brock!
Go hang yourself, you smelly badger!

MALVOLIO
[Reads]
I may command where I adore;   95
I may command who I adore

But silence, like a Lucrece knife,
But must stay silent, like a knife

With bloodless stroke my heart doth gore:
that's murdered one like me before;

M, O, A, I, doth sway my life.
M.O.A.I. doth sway my life.

FABIAN
A fustian riddle!
A made-up, gibberish riddle!

SIR TOBY BELCH
Excellent wench, say I.   100
Outstanding work, my dear, I say.

MALVOLIO
'M, O, A, I, doth sway my life.' Nay, but first,
"M.O.A.I. doth sway my life." But, first,

let me see, let me see, let me see.
well, let me see; well, let me see.

FABIAN
What dish o' poison has she dressed him!
Oh, what a poisoned chalice she has made him!

SIR TOBY BELCH
And with what wing the staniel cheques at it!
And see how fast the kestrel takes the bait!

MALVOLIO
'I may command where I adore.' Why, she may   105
"I may command where I adore." Well, she

command me: I serve her; she is my lady. Why, this
commands me; and I serve my lady. Well, this

is evident to any formal capacity; there is no
is obvious to normal minds. There's nothing

obstruction in this: and the end,--what should
to doubt about this. And the ending...what does

that alphabetical position portend? If I could make
the order of those letters mean? If I could

that resemble something in me,--Softly! M, O, A, I,--   *110*
tie them to me...hold on! "M.O.I.A"...

SIR TOBY BELCH
O, ay, make up that: he is now at a cold scent.
Go on now, make it up. He's struggling.

FABIAN
Sowter will cry upon't for all this, though it be as
This stupid hound will claim he understands,

rank as a fox.
despite the plan is reeking of deception.

MALVOLIO
M,--Malvolio; M,--why, that begins my name.
"M"—Malvolio. My name begins with M!

FABIAN
Did not I say he would work it out? The cur is   *115*
Did I not say he'd work it out? That dog

excellent at faults.
is good at finding clues, you know.

MALVOLIO
M,--but then there is no consonancy in the sequel;
"M." But, after, there's no continuity

that suffers under probation A should follow but O does.
in lettering. "A" should follow, but it's "O."

FABIAN
And O shall end, I hope.
And "ohh" will end it all, I hope.

SIR TOBY BELCH
Ay, or I'll cudgel him, and make him cry O!   *120*
Yes, or I'll clobber him and make him cry 'Oh!"

MALVOLIO
And then I comes behind.
And then "I" comes afterwards.

FABIAN
Ay, an you had any eye behind you, you might see
Yes; if you looked behind you, you'd observe

more detraction at your heels than fortunes before you.
the trick that we are playing, not good fortune.

MALVOLIO
M, O, A, I; this simulation is not as the former: and   *125*
"M.O.A.I." This code is different, but if

yet, to crush this a little, it would bow to me, for
I mix it up, it then becomes about me, for

every one of these letters are in my name.
then every letter is within my name.

Soft! Here follows prose.
Hold on, there is more writing:

[Reads]
'If this fall into thy hand, revolve. In my stars I
"If you find this, then turn it over. In rank

am above thee; but be not afraid of greatness: some   *130*
I am above you, but do not fear greatness. Some

are born great, some achieve greatness, and some
are born great, some achieve greatness, and some

have greatness thrust upon 'em. Thy Fates open
have greatness thrust upon them. Good fortune shines

their hands; let thy blood and spirit embrace them;
on you; embrace it with your mind and body,

and, to inure thyself to what thou art like to be,
And so, prepare for who you will become,

cast thy humble slough and appear fresh.   *135*
discarding all your lowly ways; be strong.

Be opposite with a kinsman, surly with servants;
Debate a gentleman, demean your servants.

let thy tongue tang arguments of state; put thyself into
Talk politics with others and then always

the trick of singularity: she thus advises thee
stand your ground. That's how the one who wants you

that sighs for thee. Remember who commended thy
hopes you'll be. Remember who admired
yellow stockings, and wished to see thee ever   140
your yellow stockings, and who wished you wore them
cross-gartered: I say, remember. Go to, thou art
criss-crossed. And remember, you will succeed
made, if thou desirest to be so; if not, let me see
if you so wish. But if you don't, just stay
thee a steward still, the fellow of servants, and
a humble servant, and mix with them, declining
not worthy to touch Fortune's fingers. Farewell.
this good fortune that's come your way. Goodbye,
She that would alter services with thee,   145
from her who'll switch to now serve you.
THE FORTUNATE-UNHAPPY.'
The lucky one who's lacking happiness."
Daylight and champaign discovers not more:
The daylight in the country's less revealing!
this is open. I will be proud, I will read politic authors,
This is so clear. I will be proud; well read;
I will baffle Sir Toby, I will wash off gross acquaintance,
I'll mystify Sir Toby; dump poor friends;
I will be point-devise the very man.
and I will be the perfect gentleman.
I do not now fool myself, to let imagination jade me;   150
I'm not fooling myself with worn imagination,
for every reason excites to this, that my lady
for all this demonstrates that my lady
loves me. She did commend my yellow stockings of late,
loves me. She complimented my yellow stockings,
she did praise my leg being cross-gartered;
and praised how I'd crossed-gartered round my leg,
and in this she manifests herself to my love,
and through this she declares her love for me,
and with a kind of injunction drives me to these habits   155
and asks that I get dressed up how she likes
of her liking. I thank my stars I am happy. I will
to see me. I'm thankful and I'm happy. I'll be

be strange, stout, in yellow stockings, and
> *brusque, in my yellow stockings, wearing them*

cross-gartered, even with the swiftness of putting on.
> *cross-gartered, which I'll put on right away.*

Jove and my stars be praised! Here is yet a
> *Good lord, I thank my lucky stars! But here's*

postscript.   160
> *another note:*

[Reads]

'Thou canst not choose but know who I am.
> *"You must have worked out who I am by now.*

If thou entertainest my love, let it appear in thy smiling;
> *If you do love me, let me know by smiling;*

thy smiles become thee well; therefore in my
> *your smile does suit you well. So, in my presence,*

presence still smile, dear my sweet, I prithee.'
> *keep smiling then, my sweet, I beg of you."*

Jove, I thank thee: I will smile; I will do   165
> *By Jove, I thank you. I will smile, whatever*

everything that thou wilt have me.
> *you want for me to do.*

[EXIT]

FABIAN
I will not give my part of this sport for a pension
> *I will not miss this even if you paid me*

of thousands to be paid from the Sophy.
> *the Shah of Persia's fortune all my life.*

SIR TOBY BELCH
I could marry this wench for this device.
> *I'd wed the woman who devised this plan.*

SIR ANDREW
So could I too.   170
> *And so would I.*

SIR TOBY BELCH
And ask no other dowry with her but such another jest.
> *I'd ask no money, just another prank.*

SIR ANDREW
Nor I neither.
I wouldn't either.

FABIAN
Here comes my noble gull-catcher.
Here comes our special catcher of the fools.

[RE-ENTER MARIA]

SIR TOBY BELCH
Wilt thou set thy foot o' my neck?
Will you stand on my neck in my submission?

SIR ANDREW
Or o' mine either?   175
Or on mine too?

SIR TOBY BELCH
Shall I play my freedom at traytrip, and become thy
Shall I roll dice to risk my freedom, losing

bond-slave?
to you and thus become a slave of yours?

SIR ANDREW
I' faith, or I either?
In truth, me too?

SIR TOBY BELCH
Why, thou hast put him in such a dream,
You've put him in a dream so magical

that when the image of it leaves him he must run mad.   180
that when he learns the truth, he will go mad.

MARIA
Nay, but say true; does it work upon him?
No, come on, speak the truth now: did it work?

SIR TOBY BELCH
Like aqua-vitae with a midwife.
Like whisky on a nurse.

MARIA
If you will then see the fruits of the sport, mark
If you desire to see the outcome, then

his first approach before my lady: he will come to
watch how he is first time he sees my lady.

her in yellow stockings, and 'tis a colour she   185
He'll come in yellow stockings; it's a colour

abhors, and cross-gartered, a fashion she detests;
she hates; cross-gartering she too detests;

and he will smile upon her, which will now be so
and he will smile at her, which, how she is now,

unsuitable to her disposition, being addicted to a
is inappropriate for how she feels,

melancholy as she is, that it cannot but turn him
for she is always sad, and it is sure

into a notable contempt. If you will see it, follow me.   190
she'll feel contempt. To see it, follow me.

SIR TOBY BELCH
To the gates of Tartar, thou most excellent devil of wit!
Off to the gates of hell, you splendid prankster!

SIR ANDREW
I'll make one too.
I'm coming too!

[EXEUNT]

ACT 3

ACT 3, SCENE 1

OLIVIA'S GARDEN.

[ENTER VIOLA, AND CLOWN WITH A TABOUR]

VIOLA
Save thee, friend, and thy music: dost thou
   God bless you and your music, friend. Do you

live by thy tabour?
   live by tabour drum?

CLOWN
No, sir, I live by the church.
   No, sir, I live by the church.

VIOLA
Art thou a churchman?
   Are you a churchman?

CLOWN
No such matter, sir: I do live by the church;   5
   Oh, no, sir, but I do live by the church,

for I do live at my house, and my house doth stand
   for I live in my house, and my house stands

by the church.
   beside the church.

VIOLA
So thou mayst say, the king lies by a beggar, if a
   So you could say the king lives by a beggar

beggar dwell near him; or, the church stands by thy
   who lives nearby; the church could be beside

tabour, if thy tabour stand by the church.   10
   your tabour if your tabour's by the church.

CLOWN
You have said, sir. To see this age!
You've got it, sir! How great to be alive!

A sentence is but a cheveril glove to a good wit:
A funny sentence is just like a glove;

how quickly the wrong side may be turned outward!
one can invert it quickly inside-out.

VIOLA
Nay, that's certain; they that dally nicely with words
Well, that's for sure. For those that play with words

may quickly make them wanton.   15
can quickly make them contradictory.

CLOWN
I would, therefore, my sister had had no name, sir.
And so I wish my sister had no name, sir.

VIOLA
Why, man?
Why, mate?

CLOWN
Why, sir, her name's a word; and to dally with that
Well, sir, her name's a word, and changing it

word might make my sister wanton. But indeed words
might make her sound promiscuous. It's true

are very rascals since bonds disgraced them.   20
that words are bad since contracts make them awful.

VIOLA
Thy reason, man?
What is your reason, mate?

CLOWN
Troth, sir, I can yield you none without words;
Sir, truly, I can't reason without words,

and words are grown so false,
and as no one believes words anymore,

I am loath to prove reason with them.
I'm loathed to reason with them.

VIOLA

I warrant thou art a merry fellow and carest for nothing.   *25*
You are a happy chap; I bet you're carefree.

CLOWN

Not so, sir, I do care for something;
Not true, dear sir, for I do care for something,

but in my conscience, sir, I do not care for you:
but if I'm honest, I don't care for you.

if that be to care for nothing, sir, I would it would make you
invisible.
For if I was carefree, you'd disappear.

VIOLA

Art not thou the Lady Olivia's fool?
Aren't you Lady Olivia's fool?

CLOWN

No, indeed, sir; the Lady Olivia has no folly: *30*
Oh no, sir, for she never wants to laugh.

she will keep no fool, sir, till she be married;
She'll have no fool until the day she's married,

and fools are as like husbands as pilchards are to herrings;
and fools to men are pilchards to a herring:

the husband's the bigger: I am indeed not
the husband's bigger. And, indeed, I'm not

her fool, but her corrupter of words.
her fool, but I corrupt her words.

VIOLA

I saw thee late at the Count Orsino's.   *35*
I saw you recently at Count Orsino's.

CLOWN

Foolery, sir, does walk about the orb like the sun,
My foolery goes round the earth, like sun

it shines every where. I would be sorry, sir, but
shines everywhere. I'm sorry, sir, but I

the fool should be as oft with your master as with
should now be with your master just as often

my mistress: I think I saw your wisdom there.
as with my mistress. Wise man, I saw you there.

VIOLA

Nay, an thou pass upon me, I'll no more with thee.   *40*

Oh no, if you make fun of me, I'll leave you.

Hold, there's expenses for thee.

Wait there, here is some money for your troubles.

CLOWN

Now Jove, in his next commodity of hair, send thee a beard!

May God—next time he gives out hair—give you a beard!

VIOLA

By my troth, I'll tell thee, I am almost sick for one;

I tell you, I am desperate for a beard,

[Aside]

though I would not have it grow on my chin.

although I do not want it on my chin.

Is thy lady within?   *45*

Is your lady inside?

CLOWN

Would not a pair of these have bred, sir?

Is there another coin from where this came from?

VIOLA

Yes, being kept together and put to use.

Yes, if invested wisely, earning interest.

CLOWN

I would play Lord Pandarus of Phrygia, sir, to bring

I'd be the go-between, like Lord Pandarus,

a Cressida to this Troilus.

to match a female coin with this here male one.

VIOLA

I understand you, sir; 'tis well begged.   *50*

I get your gist now, sir. You've begged it well.

CLOWN

The matter, I hope, is not great, sir, begging but a beggar:

It's no big deal, sir, begging from a beggar,

Cressida was a beggar. My lady

for Cressida—this coin—once begged. My lady

is within, sir. I will construe to them whence you come;

is inside; I will tell her where you've come from.

who you are and what you would are out of my welkin,
Your name and business are beyond my remit;

I might say 'element', but the word is over-worn.   55
I could say "element", but that's too common.

[EXIT]

VIOLA

This fellow is wise enough to play the fool;
This chap is smart enough to act the fool,

And to do that well craves a kind of wit:
And acting well requires intelligence.

He must observe their mood on whom he jests,
He must assess the mood of those he mocks,

The quality of persons, and the time,
The type of person, and the time of day,

And, like the haggard, cheque at every feather   60
And, like an untrained hawk, avoid distraction,

That comes before his eye. This is a practise
Retaining focus on his task. This skill

As full of labour as a wise man's art
Is just as hard as every wise man's job;

For folly that he wisely shows is fit;
For telling jokes this well is difficult;

But wise men, folly-fall'n, quite taint their wit.
When wise men's jokes fall flat, it leaves them scarred.

[ENTER SIR TOBY BELCH, AND SIR ANDREW]

SIR TOBY BELCH

Save you, gentleman.   65
Good day, gentleman.

VIOLA

And you, sir.
Good day to you, sir.

SIR ANDREW

Dieu vous garde, monsieur.
Dieu vous garde, monsieur.

VIOLA

Et vous aussi; votre serviteur.

Et vous aussi. Votre serviteur!

SIR ANDREW

I hope, sir, you are; and I am yours.

I hope you are, sir; I am yours as well.

SIR TOBY BELCH

Will you encounter the house? My niece   70

Will you be entering the house? My niece

is desirous you should enter, if your trade be to her.

is very keen, if that is why you're here.

VIOLA

I am bound to your niece, sir; I mean, she is the

I'm heading for your niece; I mean she is

list of my voyage.

the final destination on my journey.

SIR TOBY BELCH

Taste your legs, sir; put them to motion.

Try out your legs, sir; put them into motion.

VIOLA

My legs do better understand me, sir, than   75

My legs stand under me far better than

I understand what you mean by bidding me taste my legs.

I understand your meaning, "try my legs".

SIR TOBY BELCH

I mean, to go, sir, to enter.

I mean, start walking, sir. Just go inside.

VIOLA

I will answer you with gait and entrance. But we

I'll answer you by walking in, although

are prevented.

there's now no need.

[ENTER OLIVIA AND MARIA]

Most excellent accomplished lady, the heavens rain   80

Most wonderfully accomplished lady, may rain

odours on you!
shower lovely odours on you!

SIR ANDREW
That youth's a rare courtier: 'Rain odours;' well.
That youth is charming; "shower lovely odours".

VIOLA
My matter hath no voice, to your own
My message is for no one else but you,

most pregnant and vouchsafed ear.
my lady, for your willing, shielded ear.

SIR ANDREW
'Odours', 'pregnant' and 'vouchsafed:'   85
"Odours", "willing", and "shielded".

I'll get 'em all three all ready.
I'll make a note of them and use them later.

OLIVIA
Let the garden door be shut, and leave me to my hearing.
Go shut the gate, and leave me here to listen.

[EXEUNT SIR TOBY BELCH, SIR ANDREW, AND MARIA]

Give me your hand, sir.
Give me your hand, sir.

VIOLA
My duty, madam, and most humble service.
Madam, of course I will; I'm at your service.

OLIVIA
What is your name?   90
What is your name?

VIOLA
Cesario is your servant's name, fair princess.
Your servant's called Cesario, sweet princess.

OLIVIA
My servant, sir! 'Twas never merry world
My servant, sir? This world has gone to pot

Since lowly feigning was called compliment:
Since fake humility's been thought as flattery.

You're servant to the Count Orsino, youth.
You're servant to the Count Orsino, boy.

VIOLA
And he is yours, and his must needs be yours: 95
And he is yours; his servants serve your needs.

Your servant's servant is your servant, madam.
Your servant's servant is your servant, ma'am.

OLIVIA
For him, I think not on him: for his thoughts,
I don't consider him my servant. Rather

Would they were blanks, rather than filled with me!
I wish he'd think of emptiness than me.

VIOLA
Madam, I come to whet your gentle thoughts
Madam, I've come to sharpen how you think

On his behalf.   100
of him.

OLIVIA
O, by your leave, I pray you,
Give me a break, I beg of you.

I bade you never speak again of him:
I told you not to speak of him again.

But, would you undertake another suit,
But if you tell me of somebody else,

I had rather hear you to solicit that
I'd rather hear you tell me that than hear

Than music from the spheres.   105
The music of the Gods.

VIOLA
Dear lady,--
Dear lady...

OLIVIA
Give me leave, beseech you. I did send,
Give me a moment, if you please. I sent,

After the last enchantment you did here,
Just after you enchanted me right here,

A ring in chase of you: so did I abuse
A ring in chase of you. It was an error

Myself, my servant and, I fear me, you: *110*
For me, my servant, and I fear, for you.

Under your hard construction must I sit,
I must incur your poor opinion of me

To force that on you, in a shameful cunning,
By tricking you in such a shameful way

Which you knew none of yours: what might you think?
Which you knew nothing of. What do you think?

Have you not set mine honour at the stake
Have you not tied my honour to a stake,

And baited it with all the unmuzzled thoughts   *115*
Just like a baited bear, and let your thoughts

That tyrannous heart can think? To one of your receiving
Bite at me out of rage? To one so smart,

Enough is shown: a cypress, not a bosom,
It must be clear. This veil, and not my chest,

Hideth my heart. So, let me hear you speak.
Conceals my heart. So, let me hear you speak.

VIOLA
I pity you.
I pity you.

OLIVIA
        That's a degree to love.   *120*
        That is a step of love.

VIOLA
No, not a grize; for 'tis a vulgar proof,
No, not a step, for it's a sorry truth

That very oft we pity enemies.
We often sympathise with enemies.

OLIVIA
Why, then, methinks 'tis time to smile again.
I know your thoughts now; I can smile again.

O, world, how apt the poor are to be proud!
It's good, although I've nothing, I'm still proud!

If one should be a prey, how much the better 125
If one must lose, it's preferable to lose to

To fall before the lion than the wolf!
A noble lion than a rabid wolf.

[Clock strikes]

The clock upbraids me with the waste of time.
The clock reproaches me for wasting time.

Be not afraid, good youth, I will not have you:
Don't worry, youth, I will not marry you.

And yet, when wit and youth is come to harvest,
But when your mind and body has matured,

Your were is alike to reap a proper man: 130
Your wife will land herself a proper man.

There lies your way, due west.
Go off that way, due west.

VIOLA

Then westward-ho! Grace and good disposition
Then westward ho! May grace and health be with

Attend your ladyship!
your Ladyship.

You'll nothing, madam, to my lord by me?
You don't want me to send my lord a message?

OLIVIA

Stay: 135
Wait there!

I prithee, tell me what thou thinkest of me.
Please, tell me what you think of me.

VIOLA

That you do think you are not what you are.
That you think you're not who you think you are.

OLIVIA

If I think so, I think the same of you.
If I think that, I think the same of you.

VIOLA

Then think you right: I am not what I am.
You've got that right. I am not who you think.

OLIVIA

I would you were as I would have you be! 140
I wish you were the way I wish you were.

VIOLA

Would it be better, madam, than I am?
Would that be better than the way I am?

I wish it might, for now I am your fool.
I wish it would, for now you ridicule me.

OLIVIA

O, what a deal of scorn looks beautiful
Oh, even when he's angry, he is gorgeous,

In the contempt and anger of his lip!
Reflected through the anger in his lips!

A murderous guilt shows not itself more soon 145
A murderer's guilt is not so evident

Than love that would seem hid: love's night is noon.
As lover's love that shines ambivalent.

Cesario, by the roses of the spring,
Cesario, by roses of the spring,

By maidhood, honour, truth and every thing,
Virginity, my truth, and everything,

I love thee so, that, maugre all thy pride,
I love you so, despite all of your pride,

Nor wit nor reason can my passion hide. 150
Although I try, I can't my passion hide.

Do not extort thy reasons from this clause,
Don't force yourself to think from what I said

For that I woo, thou therefore hast no cause,
That though I woo you, we cannot be wed;

But rather reason thus with reason fetter,
But rather, challenge reason by the letter:

Love sought is good, but given unsought better.
Love sought is good, but love unsought is better.

VIOLA

By innocence I swear, and by my youth 155
Through innocence I swear, and through my youth

I have one heart, one bosom and one truth,
I only have one heart and have one truth;

And that no woman has; nor never none
No woman's had it, and there'll never be

Shall mistress be of it, save I alone.
A woman who will own it, only me.

And so adieu, good madam: never more
And so goodbye, madam; and nevermore

Will I my master's tears to you deplore.   *160*
Will I my master's tears to you deplore.

OLIVIA

Yet come again; for thou perhaps mayst move
But come again, in case your heart might alter

That heart, which now abhors, to like his love.
To be like his; then love will never falter.

[EXEUNT]

ACT 3, SCENE 2

OLIVIA'S HOUSE.

[ENTER SIR TOBY BELCH, SIR ANDREW, AND FABIAN]

SIR ANDREW
No, faith, I'll not stay a jot longer.
I tell you, I won't stay a second longer.

SIR TOBY BELCH
Thy reason, dear venom, give thy reason.
Oh, venomous one, do please tell me why.

FABIAN
You must needs yield your reason, Sir Andrew.
You have to share your reasoning, Sir Andrew.

SIR ANDREW
Marry, I saw your niece do more favours to the
I swear I saw your niece be friendlier

count's serving-man than ever she bestowed upon me;   5
to Count Orsino's servant than to me.

I saw't i' the orchard.
I saw it in the orchard.

SIR TOBY BELCH
Did she see thee the while, old boy? Tell me that.
Did she see you there, Andrew? Tell me that.

SIR ANDREW
As plain as I see you now.
She saw me just as well as I see you now.

FABIAN
This was a great argument of love in her toward you.
So that suggests it shows her love for you.

SIR ANDREW
'Slight, will you make an ass o' me?   10
By God's light, do you take me for a fool?

FABIAN
I will prove it legitimate, sir, upon the oaths of
I'll prove it's true, and reasoning and judgement
judgment and reason.
will swear an oath it's true.

SIR TOBY BELCH
And they have been grand-jury-men since before
For reasoning and judgement are the jury
Noah was a sailor.
since Noah built his ark.

FABIAN
She did show favour to the youth in your sight only   15
She only showed an interest in the youth
to exasperate you, to awake your dormouse valour,
to make you jealous, just to prick your courage,
to put fire in your heart and brimstone in your liver.
to stoke your heart and sulphurise your liver.
You should then have accosted her; and with some
You should have flirted with her, and with humour,
excellent jests, fire-new from the mint, you should
told cracking gags, like newly minted coins,
have banged the youth into dumbness.   20
to knock the youth to incapacitation.
This was looked for at your hand, and this was balked:
She looked for this in you, but yet you blew it.
the double gilt of this opportunity you let time wash off,
You screwed your gilt-edge opportunity
and you are now sailed into the north of my
and now you've drifted off into a memory
lady's opinion; where you will hang like an icicle
she has, where you will hang like icicles
on a Dutchman's beard, unless you do redeem it by   25
upon a Dutchman's beard, unless you do

some laudable attempt either of valour or policy.
a brave or cunning thing.

SIR ANDREW
An't be any way, it must be with valour; for policy
I must be brave; I'd hate to be thought cunning.
I hate: I had as lief be a Brownist as a politician.
I'd sooner be a puritan than conman.

SIR TOBY BELCH
Why, then, build me thy fortunes upon the basis
Why, then, go change your fortune with an act

of valour. Challenge me the count's youth to fight   *30*
of valour. Challenge Orsino's youth to fight

with him; hurt him in eleven places:
with you and hurt him in eleven places.

my niece shall take note of it; and assure thyself,
My niece will notice you, and let me tell you,

there is no love-broker in the world can more prevail
there's nothing in the world that brokers love

in man's commendation with woman than report of valour.
for women more than men who are courageous.

FABIAN
There is no way but this, Sir Andrew.   *35*
You have no other choices left, Sir Andrew.

SIR ANDREW
Will either of you bear me a challenge to him?
Will either of you take my challenge to him?

SIR TOBY BELCH
Go, write it in a martial hand; be curst and brief;
Go write it in a warlike style. Be short

it is no matter how witty, so it be eloquent and fun
and rude. Try not to make it witty but keep

of invention: taunt him with the licence of ink:
it smart, and tease him with your feisty words.

if thou thou'st him some thrice, it shall not be   *40*
And if you patronise him more than three times,

amiss; and as many lies as will lie in thy sheet of
that's not a problem; write as many lies

105

paper, although the sheet were big enough for the
as fit upon the paper, like the sheet

bed of Ware in England, set 'em down: go, about it.
had come from England's largest bed. Get going.

Let there be gall enough in thy ink, though thou
Let everything you write be full of anger,

write with a goose-pen, no matter: about it.   45
despite the fact you use a jester's pen.

SIR ANDREW
Where shall I find you?
Where shall I find you once I've written it?

SIR TOBY BELCH
We'll call thee at the cubiculo: go.
We'll call you from the bedroom. Off you go.

[EXIT SIR ANDREW]

FABIAN
This is a dear manikin to you, Sir Toby.
He's like your precious puppet now, Sir Toby.

SIR TOBY BELCH
I have been dear to him, lad, some two thousand strong,
I've spent his precious cash, two thousand times

or so.   50
at least.

FABIAN
We shall have a rare letter from him:
We'll get a classic letter out of him.

but you'll not deliver't?
But will you not deliver it?

SIR TOBY BELCH
Never trust me, then; and by all means stir on the
If not, then never trust me. I'll incite

youth to an answer. I think oxen and wainropes
the youth to answer. Oxen pulling carts

cannot hale them together. For Andrew,   55
could not drag them together. For Sir Andrew,

if he were opened, and you find so much blood
if he were opened up and there was blood

in his liver as will clog the foot of a flea, I'll eat
enough to fill a flea's foot, I would eat

the rest of the anatomy.
his corpse.

FABIAN
And his opposite, the youth, bears in his visage
And his opponent, that young chap, appears

no great presage of cruelty.   60
to not over-exude barbarity.

[ENTER MARIA]

SIR TOBY BELCH
Look, where the youngest wren of nine comes.
Here comes my little birdie.

MARIA
If you desire the spleen, and will laugh yourself
If you'd all like a giggle, one to make

into stitches, follow me. Yond gull Malvolio
you laugh in stitches, follow me. Malvolio,

is turned heathen, a very renegado;
that silly fool, has just denounced his faith,

for there is no Christian, that means to be saved by   65
because no Christian hoping for salvation

believing rightly, can ever believe such impossible passages
could possibly believe such lunacy.

of grossness. He's in yellow stockings.
He's wearing yellow stockings!

SIR TOBY BELCH
And cross-gartered?
Are they criss-crossed?

MARIA
Most villanously; like a pedant that keeps a school
Appallingly, much like a pompous teacher

i' the church. I have dogged him, like his   70
hosts classes in the church. I've plagued him like

murderer. He does obey every point of the letter
I'll ambush him. He's followed every letter

that I dropped to betray him: he does smile his
that I said he should do. He smiles so much,

face into more lines than is in the new map with the
his face has more lines on it than the new map

augmentation of the Indies: you have not seen such
of all the Eastern Indies. You've not seen

a thing as 'tis. I can hardly forbear hurling things at him.   75
a thing like this. I want to throw stuff at him.

I know my lady will strike him:
I know my lady's going to hit him soon,

if she do, he'll smile and take't for a great favour.
and when she does, he'll think she's only flirting.

SIR TOBY BELCH
Come, bring us, bring us where he is.
Come on, lead all of us to where he is.

[EXEUNT]

108

ACT 3, SCENE 3

A STREET.

[ENTER SEBASTIAN AND ANTONIO]

SEBASTIAN
I would not by my will have troubled you;
It wasn't my intention troubling you,

But, since you make your pleasure of your pains,
But, since it seems you like what you are doing,

I will no further chide you.
I will not criticise you anymore.

ANTONIO
I could not stay behind you: my desire,
I couldn't stay behind once you had gone.

More sharp than filed steel, did spur me forth;   5
My wish, as sharp as steel, did spur me onwards

And not all love to see you, though so much
And wasn't just for love of seeing you,

As might have drawn one to a longer voyage,
Although for love I'd take a longer trip,

But jealousy what might befall your travel,
But anxiously I worried for your travels,

Being skilless in these parts; which to a stranger,
For you don't know these parts, and to a stranger,

Unguided and unfriended, often prove   10
Without a guide or friend, can often seem

Rough and unhospitable: my willing love,
Rough and unfriendly. So my willing love,

The rather by these arguments of fear,
More motivated out of fear for you,

Set forth in your pursuit.
Set off in your pursuit.

SEBASTIAN
My kind Antonio,
My kind Antonio,

I can no other answer make but thanks, 15
I've nothing else to say but thanks a lot;

And thanks; and ever [ ] oft good turns
My thanks, eternal thanks. Good deeds are often

Are shuffled off with such uncurrent pay:
Fobbed off with words of thanks, instead of cash.

But, were my worth as is my conscience firm,
But if my purse was full, just like my conscience,

You should find better dealing. What's to do?
You'd get a better deal. What shall we do?

Shall we go see the reliques of this town? 20
Shall we explore this town's old monuments?

ANTONIO
To-morrow, sir: best first go see your lodging.
Let's go tomorrow. First, let's see your room.

SEBASTIAN
I am not weary, and 'tis long to night:
I am not tired; night is a long way off.

I pray you, let us satisfy our eyes
I beg you, let's both feast our eyes upon

With the memorials and the things of fame
The monuments and special things to see

That do renown this city. 25
What make this city famous.

ANTONIO
Would you'ld pardon me;
Please excuse me.

I do not without danger walk these streets:
I'm not devoid of danger on these streets.

Once, in a sea-fight, 'gainst the count his galleys
I once fought in a sea fight with the Count

I did some service; of such note indeed,
Against his ships; I did so well I fear

That were I ta'en here it would scarce be answered.   *30*
That if they captured me, I'd be defenceless.

SEBASTIAN
Belike you slew great number of his people.
So did you kill a whole load of his people?

ANTONIO
The offence is not of such a bloody nature;
It wasn't such a bloody fight as that,

Albeit the quality of the time and quarrel
Although the time and nature of our fight

Might well have given us bloody argument.
Could easily have ended in a bloodbath.

It might have since been answered in repaying   *35*
It might have since been settled through repayment

What we took from them; which, for traffic's sake,
Of what we took from them, for sake of trade,

Most of our city did: only myself stood out;
Which most folk did. But I refused to pay it,

For which, if I be lapsed in this place,
For which, if I'm caught napping in this place,

I shall pay dear.
I will pay dearly for.

SEBASTIAN
                    Do not then walk too open.   *40*
                    Don't walk outside then.

ANTONIO
It doth not fit me. Hold, sir, here's my purse.
It's not a good idea. Wait, here's my purse.

In the south suburbs, at the Elephant,
The Elephant hotel, south of the city,

Is best to lodge: I will bespeak our diet,
Will be the best to stay at. I'll get food,

Whiles you beguile the time and feed your knowledge
While you can take your time and learn about

With viewing of the town: there shall you have me.   *45*
The sights within the town. I'll meet you there.

SEBASTIAN
Why I your purse?
Why give me all your money?

ANTONIO
Haply your eye shall light upon some toy
Perhaps you'll spot something that's really nice
You have desire to purchase; and your store,
That you would like to buy, but your own funds,
I think, is not for idle markets, sir.
I think, are insufficient for this place, sir.

SEBASTIAN
I'll be your purse-bearer and leave you   50
I'll take care of your wallet, and I'll leave you
For an hour.
For an hour.

ANTONIO
To the Elephant.
The Elephant hotel.

SEBASTIAN
I do remember.
I got it.

[EXEUNT]

ACT 3, SCENE 4

OLIVIA'S GARDEN.

[ENTER OLIVIA AND MARIA]

OLIVIA
I have sent after him: he says he'll come;
I've sent for him; but if he says he'll come,

How shall I feast him? What bestow of him?
How shall I feed him? What should I give him?

For youth is bought more oft than begged or borrowed.
The young are often bought, not begged or borrowed.

I speak too loud.
I speak too loudly.

Where is Malvolio? He is sad and civil,   5
Where's Malvolio? He's miserable

And suits well for a servant with my fortunes:
And that's appropriate, a servant with my feelings.

Where is Malvolio?
Where is Malvolio?

MARIA
He's coming, madam; but in very strange manner.
He's coming, madam, but he's rather odd.

He is, sure, possessed, madam.
I'm sure he is possessed with madness, madam.

OLIVIA
Why, what's the matter? Does he rave?   10
Why, what's the matter? Is he talking nonsense?

MARIA
No, madam, he does nothing but smile:
No, madam; he does nothing else but smile.

your ladyship were best to have some guard about you,
Your ladyship should be a little cautious

if he come; for, sure, the man is tainted in's wits.
if he comes by, for he seems maladjusted.

OLIVIA
Go call him hither.
Go call him in.

[EXIT MARIA]

I am as mad as he,   15
We're both equally mad,

If sad and merry madness equal be.
If being madly happy's being sad.

[RE-ENTER MARIA, WITH MALVOLIO]

How now, Malvolio!
What's up, Malvolio?

MALVOLIO
Sweet lady, ho, ho.
Sweet lady, ho ho!

OLIVIA
Smilest thou?
What's with the smile?

I sent for thee upon a sad occasion.   20
I asked you here in sadness.

MALVOLIO
Sad, lady! I could be sad: this does make some
In sadness, lady? Yes, I could be sad,

obstruction in the blood, this cross-gartering;
for these cross-gartered laces block the blood,

but what of that? If it please the eye of one,
but who would care? For if it pleases one,

it is with me as the very true sonnet is, 'Please one, and
for me it's from that sonnet: "Please one, and

please all.'   25
please all."

OLIVIA
Why, how dost thou, man? What is the matter with thee?
Well, what on earth, man? What is wrong with you?

MALVOLIO
Not black in my mind, though yellow in my legs.
There's nothing wrong, although my legs are yellow.

It did come to his hands, and commands shall be executed:
This letter came to me, and I've obeyed it.

I think we do know the sweet Roman hand.
I think we both identify the writing.

OLIVIA
Wilt thou go to bed, Malvolio? 30
Will you go to bed, Malvolio?

MALVOLIO
To bed! Ay, sweet-heart, and I'll come to thee.
To bed? Oh, yes, my sweet; I'll come to you.

OLIVIA
God comfort thee! Why dost thou smile so and kiss
Good heavens! What is with that smile of yours,

thy hand so oft?
and what is all that kissing of your hand?

MARIA
How do you, Malvolio?
How are you, Malvolio?

MALVOLIO
At your request! Yes; nightingales answer daws. 35
D'you think I'll answer you? Me talk to crows?!

MARIA
Why appear you with this ridiculous boldness before my
lady?
What's with the bold ridiculousness before her?

MALVOLIO
'Be not afraid of greatness:' 'twas well writ.
"Be not afraid of greatness." They were wise words.

OLIVIA
What meanest thou by that, Malvolio?
What do you mean by that, Malvolio?

115

MALVOLIO
'Some are born great,'--
"Some are born great..."

OLIVIA
Ha!   40
What?

MALVOLIO
'Some achieve greatness,'--
"Some achieve greatness..."

OLIVIA
What sayest thou?
What are you saying?

MALVOLIO
'And some have greatness thrust upon them.'
"And some have greatness thrust upon them."

OLIVIA
Heaven restore thee!
Dear heaven, make him healthy!

MALVOLIO
'Remember who commended thy yellow stockings,'--   45
"Remember who admired my yellow stockings..."

OLIVIA
Thy yellow stockings!
Your yellow stockings?

MALVOLIO
'And wished to see thee cross-gartered.'
"And asked to see them criss-crossed."

OLIVIA
Cross-gartered!
Criss-crossed?

MALVOLIO
'Go to thou art made, if thou desirest to be so;'--
"Well then, you will succeed if you so wish."

OLIVIA
Am I made?   50
Have I succeeded?

116

MALVOLIO
'If not, let me see thee a servant still.'
"But if you don't, just stay a humble servant."

OLIVIA
Why, this is very midsummer madness.
It seems you've suddenly gone quite insane.

[ENTER SERVANT]

SERVANT
Madam, the young gentleman of the Count Orsino's
Madam, the young man working for Orsino

is returned: I could hardly entreat him back:
is back again. I barely kept him out.

he attends your ladyship's pleasure.   55
He wants to see your Ladyship again.

OLIVIA
I'll come to him.
I'll come to him.

[EXIT SERVANT]

Good Maria, let this fellow be looked to. Where's
Maria, take care of this fellow. Where's.

my cousin Toby? Let some of my people have a special
my cousin Toby? Have some people specially

care of him: I would not have him miscarry for the
take care of him. I wouldn't want him harmed

half of my dowry.   60
for half my dowry.

[EXEUNT OLIVIA AND MARIA]

MALVOLIO
O, ho! do you come near me now? No worse man than
Well, do you get me now? She sent no less

Sir Toby to look to me! This concurs directly with
than Sir Toby to protect me, which is

the letter: she sends him on purpose, that I may
just as her letter said. He's here on purpose

appear stubborn to him; for she incites me to that
so I can treat him rudely as she states

in the letter. 'Cast thy humble slough', says she;   65
within her letter: "Discard your lowly ways", she said.

'be opposite with a kinsman, surly with servants;
"Debate a gentleman, demean your servants,

let thy tongue tang with arguments of state;
and get engaged in talks of politics;

put thyself into the trick of singularity;' and
and always stand your ground." And then she said

consequently sets down the manner how; as, a sad
exactly how I should behave: be sombre,

face, a reverend carriage, a slow tongue, in the   70
and speak in a distinguished, tardy manner,

habit of some sir of note, and so forth. I have
just like a famous lord, or the like. I have

limed her; but it is Jove's doing, and Jove make me
seduced her, but it's the work of God, so make me

thankful! And when she went away now, 'Let this
thankful! And when she left, she said, "care for

fellow be looked to:' fellow! not Malvolio, nor
this fellow." She called me "fellow", not Malvolio!

after my degree, but fellow. Why, every thing   75
She didn't call me servant, but a fellow!

adheres together, that no dram of a scruple,
It all adds up, and not a drop of doubt,

no scruple of a scruple, no obstacle, no incredulous
not even just a tiny drop, there's no chance

or unsafe circumstance--What can be said? Nothing
this isn't true. What can I say? There's nothing

that can be can come between me and the full
that possibly could happen to prevent

prospect of my hopes. Well, Jove, not I, is the   80
my hopes from coming true. But this is God,

doer of this, and he is to be thanked.
not me, who must be thanked.

[RE-ENTER MARIA, WITH SIR TOBY BELCH AND FABIAN]

SIR TOBY BELCH
Which way is he, in the name of sanctity? If all the devils
In God's name, where is he? If all the devils
of hell be drawn in little, and Legion himself
merged with a Roman army and were shrunk
possessed him, yet I'll speak to him.
into his heart, I still would speak to him.

FABIAN
Here he is, here he is. How is't with you, sir?   85
He's here. He's here. How are you doing, sir?
How is't with you, man?
What's up with you, mate?

MALVOLIO
Go off; I discard you: let me enjoy my private: go off.
Clear off, I do not want you. Leave me be.

MARIA
Lo, how hollow the fiend speaks within him!
The devil's speaking empty words within him!
Did not I tell you? Sir Toby, my lady prays you to
I told you so! My lady asks, Sir Toby,
have a care of him.   90
you take good care of him.

MALVOLIO
Ah, ha! Does she so?
A-ha, well does she now?

SIR TOBY BELCH
Go to, go to; peace, peace; we must deal gently
Hold on, hold on! Be quiet. We have to treat him
with him: let me alone. How do you, Malvolio?
gently. Leave me with him. How's things, Malvolio?
How is't with you? What, man! Defy the devil:
How are you doing? Kick out the devil;
consider, he's an enemy to mankind.   95
he's our enemy.

MALVOLIO
Do you know what you say?
Have you any idea what you are saying?

MARIA
La you, an you speak ill of the devil, how he takes
Did you hear that? If you speak of the devil,

it at heart! Pray God, he be not bewitched!
he takes it personally! God, don't bewitch him!

FABIAN
Carry his water to the wise woman.
Have his pee examined by a white witch!

MARIA
Marry, and it shall be done to-morrow morning,   *100*
Indeed, we'll get it done tomorrow morning

if I live. My lady would not lose him for more than I'll say.
if I'm alive. My lady wants to keep him.

MALVOLIO
How now, mistress!
What do you mean?

MARIA
O Lord!
Oh Lord!

SIR TOBY BELCH
Prithee, hold thy peace; this is not the way:
Be quiet, this is not the way to treat him.

do you not see you move him? Let me alone with him.   *105*
Don't you see you're upsetting him? Leave me with him.

FABIAN
No way but gentleness; gently, gently: the fiend is
You must be gentle with him; the devil

rough, and will not be roughly used.
is rough, but don't be rough with him.

SIR TOBY BELCH
Why, how now, my bawcock! How dost thou, chuck?
What's up now, cockerel? How ya doin', chicken?

MALVOLIO
Sir!
Sir!

SIR TOBY BELCH
Ay, Biddy, come with me. What, man! 'Tis not for   *110*
Ah, baby hen, come with me. It's unwise

gravity to play at cherry-pit with Satan:
to play such childish contests with the devil.

hang him, foul collier!
Get rid of him, he's just a dirty coalman!

MARIA
Get him to say his prayers, good Sir Toby, get him to pray.
Get him to say his prayers, Sir Toby; have him pray.

MALVOLIO
My prayers, minx!
My prayers, you silly wench?

MARIA
No, I warrant you, he will not hear of godliness.   *115*
I tell you what, he will not hear of God.

MALVOLIO
Go, hang yourselves all! You are idle shallow
Go hang yourselves, the lot of you! You're lazy

things: I am not of your element:
and insignificant. I'm not like you.

you shall know more hereafter.
You'll come to learn more soon.

[EXIT]

SIR TOBY BELCH
Is't possible?
Is this really happening?

FABIAN
If this were played upon a stage now,   *120*
If this were acted out upon a stage,

I could condemn it as an improbable fiction.
I'd call it all implausibly fictitious.

SIR TOBY BELCH
His very genius hath taken the infection of the device, man.
He's taken this deception to his heart.

MARIA
Nay, pursue him now, lest the device take air and taint.
Let's follow him, in case he smells a rat.

FABIAN
Why, we shall make him mad indeed.
We're going to drive him totally insane.

MARIA
The house will be the quieter. 125
This house will then be quieter.

SIR TOBY BELCH
Come, we'll have him in a dark room and bound.
Let's tie him up and leave him in a dark room.

My niece is already in the belief that he's mad:
My niece already thinks that he is mad.

we may carry it thus, for our pleasure and his penance,
We'll do this for our pleasure and his pain

till our very pastime, tired out of breath, prompt
until we've had enough and we decide to

us to have mercy on him: at which time we will 130
take pity on him, then we can declare

bring the device to the bar and crown thee for a
in front of judge and jury that you are

finder of madmen. But see, but see.
a maker of insanity. Look out!

[ENTER SIR ANDREW]

FABIAN
More matter for a May morning.
Here's someone else to turn into a fool.

SIR ANDREW
Here's the challenge, read it: warrant there's
Read this, my letter challenging the youth.

vinegar and pepper in't. 135
It's spiced with vinegar and pepper.

FABIAN
Is't so saucy?
Is it aggressive and insulting too?

SIR ANDREW
Ay, is't, I warrant him: do but read.
Oh yes it is, I tell you. Have a read.

SIR TOBY BELCH
Give me.
Give it to me.

[Reads]
'Youth, whatsoever thou art, thou art but a scurvy fellow.'
"Young man, to me you're nothing but a scumbag."

FABIAN
Good, and valiant.   140
Good, and courageous.

SIR TOBY BELCH
[Reads]
'Wonder not, nor admire not in thy mind,
"Don't bother contemplating in your mind

why I do call thee so, for I will show thee no reason for't.'
why I would call you this; I won't reveal it."

FABIAN
A good note; that keeps you from the blow of the law.
A good note, on the right side of the law.

SIR TOBY BELCH
[Reads]
Thou comest to the lady Olivia, and in my
"You come to see Lady Olivia,

sight she uses thee kindly: but thou liest in thy throat;   145
and she is kind. But you're a lying dog,

that is not the matter I challenge thee for.'
although that is not why I challenge you."

FABIAN
Very brief, and to exceeding good sense--less.
It's short and sweet. It's sickly sweet.

SIR TOBY BELCH
[Reads]
'I will waylay thee going home; where if it
"I'll intercept you when you're heading home,

be thy chance to kill me,'--
and if you have a chance to murder me..."

FABIAN
Good.   150
Good.

SIR TOBY BELCH
[Reads]
'Thou killest me like a rogue and a villain.'
"...just kill me like an enemy of yours."

FABIAN
Still you keep o' the windy side of the law: good.
You're keeping on the right side of the law. Good.

SIR TOBY BELCH
[Reads]
'Fare thee well; and God have mercy upon
"Goodbye, and may God pardon one of us.

one of our souls! He may have mercy upon mine; but
He may have mercy on me, but I feel

my hope is better, and so look to thyself.   155
I have the better chance, so pray yourself.

Thy friend, as thou usest him, and thy sworn enemy,
Your friend, and if you choose, your enemy,

Andrew Aguecheek.
Andrew Aguecheek."

If this letter move him not, his legs cannot:
If this won't move him, then his legs won't neither.

I'll give't him.
I'll give it to him.

MARIA
You may have very fit occasion for't: he is now in   156
You might just have the chance to do that now.

some commerce with my lady, and will by and by depart.
He's talking with my lady; soon, he's leaving.

SIR TOBY BELCH
Go, Sir Andrew: scout me for him at the corner the
Go on, Sir Andrew, keep a watch for me

orchard like a bum-baily: so soon as ever thou seest
beside the orchard, like a debt-collector.

him, draw; and, as thou drawest swear horrible;
And when you see him, draw your sword and swear

for it comes to pass oft that a terrible oath,   *165*
the worst you can, for often awful words

with a swaggering accent sharply twanged off,
spat out in anger with a swaggering twang

gives manhood more approbation than ever
makes people think you're tougher than you are,

proof itself would have earned him. Away!
without the need to prove it. On your way!

SIR ANDREW
Nay, let me alone for swearing.
Don't worry, I am bloody good at swearing.

[EXIT]

SIR TOBY BELCH
Now will not I deliver his letter: for the behaviour   *170*
Now I won't send his letter, for the conduct

of the young gentleman gives him out to be of good
of that young man implies that he's a good

capacity and breeding; his employment between his
man and well bred; his interactions with

lord and my niece confirms no less: therefore this
his lord and with my niece confirm that. And so,

letter, being so excellently ignorant, will breed no
this letter—such an idiotic note—won't

terror in the youth: he will find it comes from a   *175*
frighten him. He will think it's written by

clodpole. But, sir, I will deliver his challenge by
a dimwit. But, sir, I'll recount the challenge

word of mouth; set upon Aguecheek a notable report
to him by word of mouth, describing Aguecheek

of valour; and drive the gentleman, as I know his
as full of courage, and convince the man

youth will aptly receive it, into a most hideous
—he's young so he'll believe it—that he's full of

opinion of his rage, skill, fury and impetuosity.   *180*
    horrific rage, and skill and he is fearless.

This will so fright them both that they will kill
    This will then scare them both so much they'll kill

one another by the look, like cockatrices.
    each other with their looks, like ancient monsters.

[RE-ENTER OLIVIA, WITH VIOLA]

FABIAN
Here he comes with your niece: give them way till
    Here he comes with your niece. Stay out the way

he take leave, and presently after him.
    till he has left, and then go after him.

SIR TOBY BELCH
I will meditate the while upon some horrid message   *185*
    I'll wait a while and conjure up some words

for a challenge.
    to say to challenge him.

[EXEUNT SIR TOBY BELCH, FABIAN, AND MARIA]

OLIVIA
I have said too much unto a heart of stone
    I've said too much to someone so cold-hearted

And laid mine honour too unchary out:
    And laid my reputation on the line.

There's something in me that reproves my fault;
    I feel ashamed for making this mistake,

But such a headstrong potent fault it is,   *190*
    But I felt such an overwhelming need

That it but mocks reproof.
    To say it, I could not contain myself.

VIOLA
With the same 'haviour that your passion bears
    It's just the same behaviour from your passion

Goes on my master's grief.
    That matches all the pain my master feels.

OLIVIA

Here, wear this jewel for me, 'tis my picture;

Here, wear this locket with my picture for me.

Refuse it not; it hath no tongue to vex you;   195

Do not say no. It's mute, so can't annoy you.

And I beseech you come again to-morrow.

And I request you come again tomorrow.

What shall you ask of me that I'll deny,

What can you ask from me that I'll refuse,

That honour saved may upon asking give?

Integrity intact, to give if asked?

VIOLA

Nothing but this; your true love for my master.

There's nothing but your love for my own master.

OLIVIA

How with mine honour may I give him that   200

How can I give him that, and keep my honour,

Which I have given to you?

When I have given it to you?

VIOLA

                                    I will acquit you.

                                    I'll let you.

OLIVIA

Well, come again to-morrow: fare thee well:

Well, come again tomorrow. Now, farewell;

A fiend like thee might bear my soul to hell.

A fiend like you might tempt my soul to hell.

[EXIT]

[RE-ENTER SIR TOBY BELCH AND FABIAN]

SIR TOBY BELCH

Gentleman, God save thee.   205

God save you, gentleman.

VIOLA

                                    And you, sir.

                                    And you, sir, too.

SIR TOBY BELCH
That defence thou hast, betake thee to't:
Unsheathe that sword of yours; you'll need to use it.

of what nature the wrongs are thou hast done him, I know
Whatever harm you've done to him, I do

not; but thy intercepter, full of despite, bloody as
not know, but your opponent—angry, bloodied

the hunter, attends thee at the orchard-end: 210
as a hunter—waits for you at the orchard.

dismount thy tuck, be yare in thy preparation,
Get out your sword, prepare yourself to fight,

for thy assailant is quick, skilful and deadly.
for your attacker's fast, and skilled, and deadly.

VIOLA
You mistake, sir; I am sure no man hath any quarrel to me:
You're wrong, sir. I'm sure no man wants to fight me.

my remembrance is very free and clear from any image
My recollection's good and I've no memory

of offence done to any man.   215
of doing any harm to anyone.

SIR TOBY BELCH
You'll find it otherwise, I assure you: therefore,
You'll find you're wrong, I tell you. So, therefore,

if you hold your life at any price, betake you to
if your life has some value, then be sure

your guard; for your opposite hath in him what
to be on guard, for your opponent has

youth, strength, skill and wrath can furnish man withal.
youth, strength, skill and wrath of any man.

VIOLA
I pray you, sir, what is he?   220
I beg your pardon, sir, but who's this man?

SIR TOBY BELCH
He is knight, dubbed with unhatched rapier and on
He's knighted by an unused blade, awarded

carpet consideration; but he is a devil in private
in ceremony, but he is a brutal

brawl: souls and bodies hath he divorced three; and
fighter in brawls. He's sliced three people open,

his incensement at this moment is so implacable,
but his resentment now is unrelenting

that satisfaction can be none but by pangs of death   225
and only can be quelled by putting people

and sepulchre. Hob, nob, is his word; give't or take't.
in coffins. "Kill, or be killed", is his motto; "give or take".

VIOLA
I will return again into the house and desire some
I will go back into the house and ask

conduct of the lady. I am no fighter.
my lady for protection. I'm no fighter.

I have heard of some kind of men that put quarrels
I've heard of men that like to start a fight

purposely on others, to taste their valour: 230
with others just to show that they are brave.

belike this is a man of that quirk.
He sounds like one of them sort.

SIR TOBY BELCH
Sir, no; his indignation derives itself out of a
Oh no, sir, for his anger has arisen

very competent injury: therefore, get you on and
from a deliberate offence. Prepare

give him his desire. Back you shall not to the house,
as he desires. Don't go back to the house,

unless you undertake that with me which with   235
unless you want to fight with me, but then

as much safety you might answer him: therefore, on,
you're safer fighting him. And so, let's go,

or strip your sword stark naked; for meddle you must,
or get your sword out now, for you must fight,

that's certain, or forswear to wear iron about you.
or else you'll never wear your sword again.

VIOLA
This is as uncivil as strange. I beseech you, do me
This is as rude as strange. I ask you find out,

this courteous office, as to know of the knight what   240
if you don't mind, by asking of the knight

my offence to him is: it is something of my
how I've offended him. I didn't mean to;

negligence, nothing of my purpose.
it wasn't my intention.

SIR TOBY BELCH
I will do so. Signior Fabian, stay you by this
I will do that. Sir Fabian, stay here

gentleman till my return.
and guard this man till I return.

[EXIT]

VIOLA
Pray you, sir, do you know of this matter?   245
I ask you, sir, do you know what has happened?

FABIAN
I know the knight is incensed against you, even to a
I know the knight is furious with you

mortal arbitrement; but nothing of the circumstance more.
so much he'll fight you to the death, but don't know why.

VIOLA
I beseech you, what manner of man is he?
What type of man is he?

FABIAN
Nothing of that wonderful promise, to read him by
He's doesn't look that brave—if one would judge him

his form, as you are like to find him in the proof   250
by how he looks—but you will soon find out

of his valour. He is, indeed, sir, the most skilful,
he's brutal. Sir, he is the most proficient

bloody and fatal opposite that you could possibly
and violent and fatal opposition

have found in any part of Illyria. Will you walk
you'll find across Illyria. Will you

towards him? I will make your peace with him if I can.
approach him? I'll appease him, if I can.

VIOLA

I shall be much bound to you for't: *255*

I'd be indebted to you if you did.

I am one that had rather go with sir priest than sir knight:

I'm more a churchman than a bitter fighter,

I care not who knows so much of my mettle.

and I don't care who knows I am a coward.

[EXEUNT]

[RE-ENTER SIR TOBY BELCH, WITH SIR ANDREW]

SIR TOBY BELCH

Why, man, he's a very devil; I have not seen such a

Why, mate, this man's the devil incarnate!

firago. I had a pass with him, rapier, scabbard and all,

A proper dragon! I'd a bout with him

and he gives me the stuck in with such a mortal motion,   *260*

to practice, and his thrust was so intense

that it is inevitable; and on the answer,

it certainly would kill you; on the counter,

he pays you as surely as your feet hit the ground they

he'd strike you just as sure as you are standing.

They say he has been fencer to the Sophy.

They say he was a fencer for the Shah of Persia.

SIR ANDREW

Pox on't, I'll not meddle with him.

Screw that! I will not touch him!

SIR TOBY BELCH

Ay, but he will not now be pacified: Fabian can   *265*

I know, but he will not now be appeased,

scarce hold him yonder.

for Fabian can hardly hold him back.

SIR ANDREW

Plague on't, an I thought he had been valiant and so

Oh, damn it! If I'd known he was so tough,

cunning in fence, I'd have seen him damned ere I'd

so good at fighting, I'd have placed a curse

have challenged him. Let him let the matter slip,
and not a challenge. Ask him to let the matter slip,

and I'll give him my horse, grey Capilet.   270
and I'll give him my horse, grey Capilet.

SIR TOBY BELCH
I'll make the motion: stand here, make a good show on't:
I'll make the offer. Wait here, looking brave.

this shall end without the perdition of souls.
This might just end without the loss of life.

[Aside]
Marry, I'll ride your horse as well as I ride you.
I'll ride your horse as well as I ride you.

[RE-ENTER FABIAN AND VIOLA]

[To FABIAN]
I have his horse to take up the quarrel:
I've got his horse if we settle the quarrel.

I have persuaded him the youth's a devil.   275
I have persuaded him the youth's a devil.

FABIAN
He is as horribly conceited of him; and pants and
He's terrified of him, and breathes aghast

looks pale, as if a bear were at his heels.
as though he had a bear hot on his heels.

SIR TOBY BELCH
[To VIOLA]
There's no remedy, sir; he will fight
There's no solution, sir, he's going to fight

with you for's oath sake: marry, he hath better
with you as he has sworn. But he's rethought

bethought him of his quarrel, and he finds that now   280
the reason for the fight, and now he finds

scarce to be worth talking of: therefore draw,
it's not worth fighting for. But draw your sword

the supportance of his vow; he protests he will not hurt you.
in honour, for he swears he will not hurt you.

VIOLA
[Aside]
Pray God defend me! A little thing would
Dear God, defend me! If the slightest thing
make me tell them how much I lack of a man.
occurs, I must reveal I'm not a man.

FABIAN
Give ground, if you see him furious.   285
Stand back if he seems furious to you.

SIR TOBY BELCH
Come, Sir Andrew, there's no remedy; the gentleman
Sir Andrew, come; there is no other way.
will, for his honour's sake, have one bout with you;
He'll, in the name of honour, fight one bout.
he cannot by the duello avoid it: but he has
The code of fighting stipulates it. But, as
promised me, as he is a gentleman and a soldier,
a gentleman and soldier, he has promised
he will not hurt you. Come on; to't.   290
that he won't hurt you. Come now, get to it.

SIR ANDREW
Pray God, he keep his oath!
I pray to God that he will keep his promise!

VIOLA
I do assure you, 'tis against my will.
I promise you this isn't what I wanted.
[They draw]

[ENTER ANTONIO]

ANTONIO
Put up your sword. If this young gentleman
Put down your sword. If this young gentleman
Have done offence, I take the fault on me:
Has done you wrong, it's me who'll take the blame.
If you offend him, I for him defy you.   295
If you've offended him, I'll fight you back.

SIR TOBY BELCH
You, sir! Why, what are you?
You, sir? Why, who are you?

ANTONIO
One, sir, that for his love dares yet do more
I am someone who, out of love, will dare
Than you have heard him brag to you he will.
To do the things you've only heard him boast of.

SIR TOBY BELCH
Nay, if you be an undertaker, I am for you.
If you do others dirty work, I'll fight you.

[They draw]

[ENTER OFFICERS]

FABIAN
O good Sir Toby, hold! Here come the officers.   300
Wait up, Sir Toby, wait! The police are here.

SIR TOBY BELCH
I'll be with you anon.
I'll get you later.

VIOLA
Pray, sir, put your sword up, if you please.
Please sir, put down your sword, if you don't mind.

SIR ANDREW
Marry, will I, sir; and, for that I promised you,
Indeed, I will. And as I promised you,
I'll be as good as my word: he will bear
I'll be good to my word. My horse will carry
you easily and reins well.   305
you easily, and he's a breeze to ride.

FIRST OFFICER
This is the man; do thy office.
This is the man. Conduct your duty on him.

SECOND OFFICER
Antonio, I arrest thee at the suit of Count Orsino.
Antonio, I arrest you under Count Orsino's order.

ANTONIO
You do mistake me, sir.
You must mistake me, sir.

FIRST OFFICER
No, sir, no jot; I know your favour well,
No, sir, no way. I know the way you look,
Though now you have no sea-cap on your head.   310
Despite the fact you're not wearing your sea-cap.
Take him away: he knows I know him well.
Take him away. He knows I know him well.

ANTONIO
I must obey.
I must obey.
[*To VIOLA*]
              This comes with seeking you:
              This happened seeking you.
But there's no remedy; I shall answer it.
There's no solution; I'll just pay the fine.
What will you do, now my necessity   315
What will you do now that I have to ask
Makes me to ask you for my purse? It grieves me
You give me back my cash? It hurts me now
Much more for what I cannot do for you
Much more for what I cannot do for you
Than what befalls myself. You stand amazed;
Than what will be my fate. You look surprised,
But be of comfort.
But just relax.

SECOND OFFICER
Come, sir, away.   320
Come on now, sir, let's go.

ANTONIO
I must entreat of you some of that money.
I have to ask you give me back some money.

VIOLA
What money, sir?
What money, sir?

For the fair kindness you have showed me here,
For all the kindness you have shown to me,

And, part, being prompted by your present trouble,
And also for the trouble you're now in,

Out of my lean and low ability   325
I can, from my own limited resources,

I'll lend you something: my having is not much;
Lend you some money. But I don't have much.

I'll make division of my present with you:
I'll give you some of what I have right now.

Hold, there's half my coffer.
Here's half of all I have.

ANTONIO
Will you deny me now?
Will you disown me now?

Is't possible that my deserts to you   330
How can you, after all I've done for you,

Can lack persuasion? Do not tempt my misery,
Not help me out? Don't make me more upset

Lest that it make me so unsound a man
In case I'm forced to do an awful thing

As to upbraid you with those kindnesses
Reminding you of all the acts of kindness

That I have done for you.
I've done for you.

VIOLA
                              I know of none;   335
I don't know any of them.

Nor know I you by voice or any feature:
And I don't know you by your face or voice.

I hate ingratitude more in a man
I hate ingratitude in men far more

Than lying, vainness, babbling, drunkenness,
Than lying, vanity, or drunkenness,

Or any taint of vice whose strong corruption
Or any other strong corrupting weakness

Inhabits our frail blood.   340
That we are subject to...

ANTONIO

O heavens themselves!
Good heavens, what on earth...!

SECOND OFFICER

Come, sir, I pray you, go.
Come on now, sir, let's go.

ANTONIO

Let me speak a little. This youth that you see here
Wait, let me say something. This youth you see

I snatched one half out of the jaws of death,
I saved from half-way down the jaws of death,

Relieved him with such sanctity of love,   *345*
And brought him comfort from the love I gave him,

And to his image, which methought did promise
And to his face, which I thought reassured me

Most venerable worth, did I devotion.
He is a decent man, I stayed devoted.

FIRST OFFICER

What's that to us? The time goes by: away!
Why should we care? Time's ticking by. Let's go.

ANTONIO

But O how vile an idol proves this god
But oh, how awful has my hero proven!

Thou hast, Sebastian, done good feature shame.   *350*
Sebastian, you've pilloried your good looks.

In nature there's no blemish but the mind;
There's nothing bad in nature, but the mind;

None can be called deformed but the unkind:
For nothing's bad except being unkind.

Virtue is beauty, but the beauteous evil
Now beauty's beautiful, but evil beauty

Are empty trunks o'erflourished by the devil.
Is just an empty shell, the devil's duty.

FIRST OFFICER

The man grows mad: away with him! Come, come, sir.   *355*
He's going mad. Take him away. Come, sir.

ANTONIO
Lead me on.
Lead me onwards.

[EXIT WITH OFFICERS]

VIOLA
Methinks his words do from such passion fly,
I think he spoke those words with so much zeal
That he believes himself: so do not I.
That he believes them, though I doubt they're real.
Prove true, imagination, O, prove true,
Oh, my imagination, please be true,
That I, dear brother, be now ta'en for you!   360
That I, dear brother, he assumed was you!

SIR TOBY BELCH
Come hither, knight; come hither, Fabian:
Let's leave here now, dear knight and Fabian.
we'll whisper o'er a couplet or two of most sage saws.
Let's share some wise old sayings with each other.

VIOLA
He named Sebastian: I my brother know
He said Sebastian. I see my brother
Yet living in my glass; even such and so
When looking in the mirror. There's no other
In favour was my brother, and he went   365
Whose face was just like mine; he wore his clothes
Still in this fashion, colour, ornament,
The same as these, in colour, shape and pose,
For him I imitate: O, if it prove,
For I would copy him. Oh, prove it so
Tempests are kind and salt waves fresh in love.
That storms are kind and waves did let him go.

[EXIT]

SIR TOBY BELCH
A very dishonest paltry boy, and more a coward than
He's such a weak, dishonest boy; a coward

a hare: his dishonesty appears in leaving his   *370*
    much like a hare. He lies, for he is leaving

friend here in necessity and denying him;
    his friend here, desperate, denying he knows him.

and for his cowardship, ask Fabian.
    And as for weakness, just ask Fabian.

FABIAN
A coward, a most devout coward, religious in it.
    A coward of quite biblical proportions.

SIR ANDREW
'Slid, I'll after him again and beat him.
    By God, I'll follow him and beat him up.

SIR TOBY BELCH
Do; cuff him soundly, but never draw thy sword.   *375*
    Give him a kicking, but don't draw your sword.

SIR ANDREW
An I do not,--
    And if I don't...

FABIAN
Come, let's see the event.
    Come on, let's see what happens.

SIR TOBY BELCH
I dare lay any money 'twill be nothing yet.
    I bet there will be nothing much to see.

[EXEUNT]

ACT 4

ACT 4, SCENE 1

BEFORE OLIVIA'S HOUSE.

[ENTER SEBASTIAN AND CLOWN]

CLOWN
Will you make me believe that I am not sent for you?
Do you want me to think you are not you?

SEBASTIAN
Go to, go to, thou art a foolish fellow:
Get lost, you silly fool.

Let me be clear of thee.
Get out of my way.

CLOWN
Well held out, i' faith! No, I do not know you; nor
Ha ha, great bluffing! No, I don't know you, nor

I am not sent to you by my lady, to bid you come   5
am I sent here by my lady asking

speak with her; nor your name is not Master Cesario;
you speak to her, nor is your name Cesario,

nor this is not my nose neither. Nothing that is so is so.
and this is not my nose. For nothing's real.

SEBASTIAN
I prithee, vent thy folly somewhere else:
Clear off; go talk your nonsense somewhere else.

Thou know'st not me.
You don't know me.

CLOWN
Vent my folly! He has heard that word of some   10
Go talk my nonsense? That's a phrase he's heard

great man and now applies it to a fool.
from someone smart, then shares it with a fool.

Vent my folly! I am afraid this great lubber, the world,
Go talk my nonsense? I'm afraid this world

will prove a cockney. I prithee now, ungird thy
is turning working class. Please now, stop acting

strangeness and tell me what I shall vent to
all strange and tell me what I ought to tell

my lady: shall I vent to her that thou art coming?   15
my lady. Shall I tell her you'll be coming?

SEBASTIAN
I prithee, foolish Greek, depart from me:
Come on, kebab-head, please be on your way.

There's money for thee: if you tarry longer, I shall give
Here's money. If you wait here longer, I'll give

worse payment.
you something worse in compensation.

CLOWN
By my troth, thou hast an open hand. These wise men
How generous of you. When wise men give

that give fools money get themselves a   20
some money to a fool, they get acclaim...

good report--after fourteen years' purchase.
...if they keep up their payments fourteen years.

[ENTER SIR ANDREW, SIR TOBY BELCH, AND FABIAN]

SIR ANDREW
Now, sir, have I met you again? There's for you.
We meet again. Here is a punch for you.

SEBASTIAN
Why, there's for thee, and there, and there.
And here's one back for you, and two and three.

Are all the people mad?
Is everybody crazy here?

SIR TOBY BELCH
Hold, sir, or I'll throw your dagger o'er the house.   25
Stop, else I'll throw your dagger past the house.

CLOWN
This will I tell my lady straight: I would not be
I'll tell my lady of this. I would not be
in some of your coats for two pence.
in your shoes if you paid me.

[EXIT]

SIR TOBY BELCH
Come on, sir; hold.
Come on, sir, stop that now.

SIR ANDREW
Nay, let him alone: I'll go another way to work
No, leave him be. I've got another way
with him; I'll have an action of battery against him,   30
to punish him. I'll charge him with assault,
if there be any law in Illyria:
and win it if Illyria has laws,
though I struck him first, yet it's no matter for that.
although I hit him first, that doesn't matter.

SEBASTIAN
Let go thy hand.
Let go of me!

SIR TOBY BELCH
Come, sir, I will not let you go. Come, my young soldier,
Come, sir. I will not let you go. Young soldier,
put up your iron: you are well fleshed; come on.   35
put down your dagger; you are strong; come on.

SEBASTIAN
I will be free from thee. What wouldst thou now?
I'll free myself from you. What will you do now?
If thou darest tempt me further, draw thy sword.
If you dare to fight me, then whip out your sword.

SIR TOBY BELCH
What, what? Nay, then I must have an ounce or two
What? No, for then I'd draw an ounce or two
of this malapert blood from you.
of your audacious blood from you.

145

[ENTER OLIVIA]

OLIVIA
Hold, Toby; on thy life I charge thee, hold!   40
Wait, Toby! Stop, upon your life, wait up!

SIR TOBY BELCH
Madam!
Madam.

OLIVIA
Will it be ever thus? Ungracious wretch,
Will you always be like this? Boorish lout,

Fit for the mountains and the barbarous caves,
You should be in a barbarous mountain cave

Where manners ne'er were preached! Out of my sight!
Where no one teaches manners! Out of here!

Be not offended, dear Cesario.   45
Don't be offended, dear Cesario.

Rudesby, be gone!
Get out of here, you ruffian!

[EXEUNT SIR TOBY BELCH, SIR ANDREW, AND FABIAN]

I prithee, gentle friend,
Sweet friend,

Let thy fair wisdom, not thy passion, sway
Let your intelligence, and not your anger,

In this uncivil and thou unjust extent
Guide you to understand this violence

Against thy peace. Go with me to my house,   50
Against your peaceful nature. Come with me

And hear thou there how many fruitless pranks
To my house and I'll tell you of the pranks

This ruffian hath botched up, that thou thereby
That ruffian screws up, so that we can

Mayst smile at this: thou shalt not choose but go:
Laugh all this off. You have to come with me.

Do not deny. Beshrew his soul for me,
Don't turn me down. For me, despise his soul!

He started one poor heart of mine in thee.   55
He scared my heart, the one that you just stole.

SEBASTIAN
What relish is in this? How runs the stream?
What's causing this? All's not as it may seem.

Or I am mad, or else this is a dream:
I'm either mad, or else this is a dream.

Let fancy still my sense in Lethe steep;
If it's a fairytale, it's one to keep;

If it be thus to dream, still let me sleep!
If it's a dream, I want to stay asleep!

OLIVIA
Nay, come, I prithee; would thou'ldst be ruled by me!   60
No, come with me, if you'll do as I ask.

SEBASTIAN
Madam, I will.
Madam, I will.

OLIVIA
                    O, say so, and so be!
                    Oh, you're up to the task!

[EXEUNT]

147

ACT 4, SCENE 2

OLIVIA'S HOUSE.

[ENTER MARIA AND CLOWN]

MARIA
Nay, I prithee, put on this gown and this beard;
No, come along, put on this gown and beard,

make him believe thou art Sir Topas the curate:
and make him think you're Sir Topas the priest.

do it quickly; I'll call Sir Toby the whilst.
Chop, chop, meanwhile I'll call Sir Toby in.

[EXIT]

CLOWN
Well, I'll put it on, and I will dissemble myself in't;
I'll wear it and disguise myself completely,

and I would I were the first that ever   5
I wish I were the first fraudster to wear

dissembled in such a gown. I am not tall enough to
a gown like this. I'm hardly fat enough to

become the function well, nor lean enough to be
look the part, nor thin enough to be

thought a good student; but to be said an honest man
a careful student, but being called an honest man

and a good housekeeper goes as fairly as to say a
and housekeeper is just as good as called

careful man and a great scholar. The competitors enter.   10
careful and smart. My conspirators are here.

[ENTER SIR TOBY BELCH AND MARIA]

148

SIR TOBY BELCH
Jove bless thee, master Parson.
God bless you, Master Parson.

CLOWN
Bonos dies, Sir Toby: for, as the old hermit
Buenos dias, Sir Toby. For, as the hermit

of Prague, that never saw pen and ink, very wittily
of Prague, who couldn't read or write, said laughing

said to a niece of King Gorboduc, 'That that is is;'
to King Gorboduc's niece, "What is, will be",

so I, being Master Parson, am Master Parson;   *15*
and so as Master Parson, I'm a parson,

for, what is 'that' but 'that', and 'is' but 'is'?
for "what" is "what", and "is" will be.

SIR TOBY BELCH
To him, Sir Topas.
Go see Malvolio, Sir Topas, now.

CLOWN
What, ho, I say! Peace in this prison!
What's happening here, I ask! Peace in this prison!

SIR TOBY BELCH
The knave counterfeits well; a good knave.
That fool disguises well. An able fool.

MALVOLIO
[Within]
Who calls there?   *20*
Who's calling out?

CLOWN
Sir Topas the curate, who comes to visit Malvolio
The priest Sir Topas, here to see Malvolio

the lunatic.
the lunatic.

MALVOLIO
Sir Topas, Sir Topas, good Sir Topas, go to my lady.
Sir Topas? Good, Sir Topas, see my lady...

CLOWN
Out, hyperbolical fiend! How vexest thou this man!
Vacate this man, foul devil! You've confused him

Talkest thou nothing but of ladies?   25
and now he talks of nothing but the ladies.

SIR TOBY BELCH
Well said, Master Parson.
Well said there, Master Pastor.

MALVOLIO
Sir Topas, never was man thus wronged:
Sir Topas, someone's never been so wronged.

good Sir Topas, do not think I am mad:
Dearest Sir Topas, do not think I'm mad.

they have laid me here in hideous darkness.
They've put me here in total darkness...

CLOWN
Fie, thou dishonest Satan! I call thee by the most   30
Quiet, you lying devil! I am speaking

modest terms; for I am one of those gentle ones
politely to you, for I am a kind man

that will use the devil himself with courtesy:
who will address the devil with decorum.

sayest thou that house is dark?
You say this place is dark?

MALVOLIO
As hell, Sir Topas.
As dark as hell, Sir Topas.

CLOWN
Why it hath bay windows transparent as barricadoes,   35
But there are windows that are clear like railings,

and the clearstores toward the south north are as
and upper windows open north and south,

lustrous as ebony; and yet complainest thou of
shine out like ebony, yet you complain

obstruction?
you can't see anything?

MALVOLIO
I am not mad, Sir Topas: I say to you, this house is dark.
Sir Topas, I'm not mad; it's dark in here.

CLOWN
Madman, thou errest: I say, there is no darkness   40
Madman, you're wrong. There is no darkness here,

but ignorance; in which thou art more puzzled than
except your ignorance; you're more confused than

the Egyptians in their fog.
wandering Egyptians in the fog.

MALVOLIO
I say, this house is as dark as ignorance, though
This house is dark as ignorance, I tell you,

ignorance were as dark as hell; and I say, there
if ignorance was as dark as hell. A man

was never man thus abused. I am no more mad than you   45
has never been so badly treated. I'm no

are: make the trial of it in any constant question.
more mad than you. So, test me with a question.

CLOWN
What is the opinion of Pythagoras concerning wild fowl?
What is Pythagoras's view of wildfowl?

MALVOLIO
That the soul of our grandam might haply inhabit a bird.
That grandma's soul might live inside a bird.

CLOWN
What thinkest thou of his opinion?
What do you think of his opinion?

MALVOLIO
I think nobly of the soul, and no way approve his opinion.   50
I respect the soul, and don't agree with him.

CLOWN
Fare thee well. Remain thou still in darkness:
Goodbye. You will remain here left in darkness.

thou shalt hold the opinion of Pythagoras ere I will
You will believe Pythagoras's views

allow of thy wits, and fear to kill a woodcock,
before you're sane, and fear to kill a bird

lest thou dispossess the soul of thy grandam. Fare thee well.
in case it is your gran. Goodbye.

MALVOLIO
Sir Topas, Sir Topas!   55
Sir Topas! Sir Topas!

SIR TOBY BELCH
My most exquisite Sir Topas!
My beautiful Sir Topas!

CLOWN
Nay, I am for all waters.
No, I can play at any given role.

MARIA
Thou mightst have done this without thy beard and gown:
You could have done that minus beard and gown.

he sees thee not.
He cannot see you.

SIR TOBY BELCH
To him in thine own voice, and bring me word how   60
Talk in your own voice to him, and tell me how

thou findest him: I would we were well rid of this
you find him. I would like to stop all this

knavery. If he may be conveniently delivered,
tomfoolery. If there's a way to stop this,

I would he were, for I am now so far in offence with
let's do so, for I'm in a lot of trouble

my niece that I cannot pursue with any safety this
already with my niece and can't continue

sport to the upshot. Come by and by to my chamber.   65
without getting in more. Come to my room soon.

[EXEUNT SIR TOBY BELCH AND MARIA]

CLOWN
[Singing]
'Hey, Robin, jolly Robin,
"Hey, Robin, jolly Robin,

Tell me how thy lady does.'
  Tell me how your lady is."

MALVOLIO
Fool!
  Fool?

CLOWN
'My lady is unkind, perdy.'
  "My lady is unkind indeed."

MALVOLIO
Fool!   70
  Fool!

CLOWN
'Alas, why is she so?'
  "Oh dear, why is she so?"

MALVOLIO
Fool, I say!
  Fool, I say!

CLOWN
'She loves another'--Who calls, ha?
  "She loves another..." Who is calling?

MALVOLIO
Good fool, as ever thou wilt deserve well at my hand,
  Good fool, I will forever treat you well
help me to a candle, and pen, ink and paper: 75
  if you give me a candle, pen, ink, and paper.
as I am a gentleman, I will live to be
  As a gentleman, I'll be forever
thankful to thee for't.
  thankful to you for that.

CLOWN
Master Malvolio?
  Master Malvolio?

MALVOLIO
Ay, good fool.
  Yes, dear fool.

CLOWN

Alas, sir, how fell you besides your five wits?   80

Oh dear, what was it made you go insane?

MALVOLIO

Fool, there was never a man so notoriously abused:

There's never been a man so badly treated.

I am as well in my wits, fool, as thou art.

I am as sane as you, dear fool.

CLOWN

But as well? Then you are mad indeed,

As sane as me? Then you are mad indeed,

if you be no better in your wits than a fool.

if you're no saner than a silly fool.

MALVOLIO

They have here propertied me; keep me in darkness,   85

They've locked me up in here, in total darkness,

send ministers to me, asses, and do all they can to

and sent me priests—the silly fools!—to make me

face me out of my wits.

go quite insane by saying that I'm mad.

CLOWN

Advise you what you say; the minister is here.

Be careful what you say. The priest is here.

Malvolio, Malvolio, thy wits the heavens restore!

Malvolio: the heavens make you sane.

Endeavour thyself to sleep, and leave thy vain   90

Try going to sleep and then stop talking all

bibble babble.

that drivel.

MALVOLIO

Sir Topas!

Sir Topas!

CLOWN

Maintain no words with him, good fellow.

Don't speak to him again, good fellow.

Who, I, sir? Not I, sir. God be wi' you, good Sir Topas.

Who me, sir? No I won't! Goodbye, Sir Topas.

Merry, amen. I will, sir, I will. 95
Well, then, amen. I will, sir, I will.

MALVOLIO
Fool, fool, fool, I say!
Fool! Fool! Fool, I say!

CLOWN
Alas, sir, be patient. What say you sir?
Yes sir, just wait. What do you want to say?

I am shent for speaking to you.
I've just been told I cannot talk to you.

MALVOLIO
Good fool, help me to some light and some paper:
Good fool, please help me get some light and paper.

I tell thee, I am as well in my wits as any man in Illyria. 100
I tell you, I'm as sane as any man here in Illyria.

CLOWN
Well-a-day that you were, sir.
Well that'll be the day, sir!

MALVOLIO
By this hand, I am. Good fool, some ink, paper and
I promise I am. Good fool, some ink, paper,

light; and convey what I will set down to my lady:
and light; and write a message to my lady.

it shall advantage thee more than ever the bearing
You'll do better delivering this than from

of letter did. 105
anything you've done before.

CLOWN
I will help you to't. But tell me true,
I'll help you with it. Tell me first the truth:

are you not mad indeed? Or do you but counterfeit?
are you not mad or are you just pretending?

MALVOLIO
Believe me, I am not; I tell thee true.
Believe me, I'm not mad. I speak the truth.

CLOWN

Nay, I'll ne'er believe a madman till I see
   I won't believe a madman till I see

his brains. I will fetch you light and paper and ink.   *110*
   his brains. I'll get a light and ink for you.

MALVOLIO

Fool, I'll requite it in the highest degree:
   Fool, I'll return the favour best I can.

I prithee, be gone.
   But get those things, be gone.

CLOWN

[Singing]

I am gone, sir,
   I am gone, sir,

And anon, sir,
   and anon, sir,

I'll be with you again,   *115*
   I'll be with you again,

In a trice,
   In a moment,

Like to the old Vice,
   an opponent,

Your need to sustain;
   You need to remain.

Who, with dagger of lath,
   Who with dagger of wood,

In his rage and his wrath,   *120*
   and up to no good,

Cries, ah, ha! to the devil:
   cries "a-ha" to the devil;

Like a mad lad,
   Like a mad lad,

Pare thy nails, dad;
   "Clip your wings, dad!

Adieu, good man devil.
   Goodbye, respectable devil."

[EXIT]

ACT 4, SCENE 3

OLIVIA'S GARDEN.

[ENTER SEBASTIAN]

SEBASTIAN
This is the air; that is the glorious sun;
This is the air and that's the lovely sun.

This pearl she gave me, I do feel't and see't;
I see and feel this pearl she gave to me.

And though 'tis wonder that enwraps me thus,
Although I am amazed at what has happened,

Yet 'tis not madness. Where's Antonio, then?
I am not mad. Where is Antonio now?

I could not find him at the Elephant: 5
He wasn't at the Elephant hotel.

Yet there he was; and there I found this credit,
He'd been there, for they told me that he'd been

That he did range the town to seek me out.
And that he'd left to scour the town for me.

His counsel now might do me golden service;
I'd love to have his sound advice right now.

For though my soul disputes well with my sense,
For though my heart and common sense agree

That this may be some error, but no madness,   10
That this is just an error, and not madness,

Yet doth this accident and flood of fortune
This chance encounter and astounding luck

So far exceed all instance, all discourse,
Are so beyond all precedent and reason,

That I am ready to distrust mine eyes
That I'm prepared to think my eyes are lying,

And wrangle with my reason that persuades me
Debating with my reason to persuade me

To any other trust but that I am mad   *15*
That there's no other cause except I'm mad.

Or else the lady's mad; yet, if 'twere so,
Or else the lady's mad. But if she's mad,

She could not sway her house, command her followers,
She would not run her house, direct her staff,

Take and give back affairs and their dispatch
Receive and process all her paperwork

With such a smooth, discreet and stable bearing
With smooth, discreet and level-headed skill,

As I perceive she does: there's something in't   *20*
As I perceive she does. Something's occurring

That is deceivable. But here the lady comes.
That's tricking me. But here she comes again.

[ENTER OLIVIA AND PRIEST]

OLIVIA
Blame not this haste of mine. If you mean well,
Don't blame me being hasty. If you love me,

Now go with me and with this holy man
Come with me now and with this holy man

Into the chantry by: there, before him,
Into this private chapel. There, before him,

And underneath that consecrated roof,   *25*
And underneath its consecrated roof,

Plight me the full assurance of your faith;
Declare that you'll be faithful unto me

That my most jealous and too doubtful soul
So that my over-jealous, doubting soul

May live at peace. He shall conceal it
Can be at peace. He's going to keep it quiet

Whiles you are willing it shall come to note,
Until you want to share the news with others;

What time we will our celebration keep   *30*
And then we'll host our wedding celebration

According to my birth. What do you say?

In line with my position. What d'you think?

SEBASTIAN

I'll follow this good man, and go with you;

I'll follow this good man and go with you,

And, having sworn truth, ever will be true.

And, when we're wed, I always will be true.

OLIVIA

Then lead the way, good father; and heavens so shine,

Then lead the way, good father; heaven's shine

That they may fairly note this act of mine!   35

Upon us, so they'll see this act of mine.

[EXEUNT]

ACT 5

ACT 5, SCENE 1

BEFORE OLIVIA'S HOUSE.

[ENTER CLOWN AND FABIAN]

FABIAN
Now, as thou lovest me, let me see his letter.
Now, if you love me, let me see his letter.

CLOWN
Good Master Fabian, grant me another request.
Good Fabian, please grant me one request.

FABIAN
Any thing.
Anything you want.

CLOWN
Do not desire to see this letter.
Don't ask to see this letter.

FABIAN
This is, to give a dog, and in recompense desire   5
That's just like gifting somebody a dog,
my dog again.
then asking for it back in compensation.

[ENTER DUKE ORSINO, VIOLA, CURIO, AND LORDS]

DUKE ORSINO
Belong you to the Lady Olivia, friends?
Are you Lady Olivia's employees?

CLOWN
Ay, sir; we are some of her trappings.
Yes, sir, we're some of them who work for her.

163

DUKE ORSINO
I know thee well; how dost thou, my good fellow?
I know you well. How are you, my good man?

CLOWN
Truly, sir, the better for my foes and the worse   10
Better because of enemies, but worse
for my friends.
because of friends, I tell you, sir.

DUKE ORSINO
Just the contrary; the better for thy friends.
That can't be right; you're better with your friends.

CLOWN
No, sir, the worse.
No, sir, I'm worse.

DUKE ORSINO
How can that be?
How can that be?

CLOWN
Marry, sir, they praise me and make an ass of me;   15
Well, sir, they praise me but make me look stupid.
now my foes tell me plainly I am an ass:
My enemies just tell me I'm a fool.
so that by my foes, sir I profit in the knowledge of myself,
And so my enemies impart real knowledge,
and by my friends, I am abused: so that,
but from my friends, it's lies. So, in conclusion,
conclusions to be as kisses, if your four negatives
if, like kisses, four negatives become
make your two affirmatives why then, the worse for   20
two positives, with friends they're always lying,
my friends and the better for my foes.
and so my friends are worse than foes.

DUKE ORSINO
Why, this is excellent.
Well, quite excellent.

CLOWN
By my troth, sir, no; though it please you to be
It's not...unless, of course, you want to be
one of my friends.
a friend of mine.

DUKE ORSINO
Thou shalt not be the worse for me: there's gold.   *25*
You won't be worse off; here's a coin from me.

CLOWN
But that it would be double-dealing, sir,
If you could give me two of them, dear sir,
I would you could make it another.
I'd have another coin.

DUKE ORSINO
O, you give me ill counsel.
You give me bad advice.

CLOWN
Put your grace in your pocket, sir, for this once,
Return your generous hand into your pocket
and let your flesh and blood obey it.   *30*
and let your hand obey my bad advice.

DUKE ORSINO
Well, I will be so much a sinner, to be a
It will be wrong of me to dip my hand
double-dealer: there's another.
again; but here's another coin for you.

CLOWN
Primo, secundo, tertio, is a good play;
A-one, a-two, a-three's a splendid game,
and the old saying is, the third pays for all:
and as the saying goes, it's third time lucky.
the triplex, sir, is a good tripping measure; or the bells of   *35*
The three-step is a splendid dance, or church bells
Saint Bennet, sir, may put you in mind; one, two, three.
might give you an idea of one, two, three.

DUKE ORSINO

You can fool no more money out of me at this throw:
You'll charm no further money out of me.

if you will let your lady know I am here
But if you let your lady know I'm here

to speak with her, and bring her along with you,
to speak to her, and bring her here yourself,

it may awake my bounty further.   40
then maybe I will make a further payment.

CLOWN

Marry, sir, lullaby to your bounty
Then, sir, your generosity can sleep

till I come again. I go, sir; but I would not have you
until I come again. I hope you don't

to think that my desire of having is the sin of covetousness:
think I am motivated just by greed.

but, as you say, sir, let your bounty take a nap,
But, as you say, let kindness take a nap;

I will awake it anon.   45
I'll wake it soon enough.

[EXIT]

VIOLA

Here comes the man, sir, that did rescue me.
Here comes the man who rescued me, my lord.

[ENTER ANTONIO AND OFFICERS]

DUKE ORSINO

That face of his I do remember well;
That face of his I do remember well.

Yet, when I saw it last, it was besmeared
But last time that I saw him, he was smeared

As black as Vulcan in the smoke of war:
In war-paint black, the work of Roman gods.

A bawbling vessel was he captain of,   50
He was the captain of a poxy boat

For shallow draught and bulk unprizable;
With shallow draught that wasn't worth a thing,

166

With which such scathful grapple did he make
But he did so much damage in the fight

With the most noble bottom of our fleet,
Against our grandest ship within the fleet

That very envy and the tongue of loss
That we were jealous, almost lost for words,

Cried fame and honour on him. What's the matter?   55
Reluctantly respecting him. What's up?

FIRST OFFICER
Orsino, this is that Antonio
Orsino, this man is Antonio;

That took the Phoenix and her fraught from Candy;
He stole the Phoenix and its freight from Crete;

And this is he that did the Tiger board,
And he's the one who got aboard the Tiger

When your young nephew Titus lost his leg:
That time your nephew Titus lost his leg.

Here in the streets, desperate of shame and state,   60
Here in the streets, with reckless disregard,

In private brabble did we apprehend him.
We apprehended him as he was fighting.

VIOLA
He did me kindness, sir, drew on my side;
He has been kind to me; he drew his sword

But in conclusion put strange speech upon me:
To fight for me, but then said something strange.

I know not what 'twas but distraction.
I can't explain it; maybe it was madness.

DUKE ORSINO
Notable pirate! thou salt-water thief!   65
You legendary pirate, ocean thief,

What foolish boldness brought thee to their mercies,
What foolish boldness made you get arrested

Whom thou, in terms so bloody and so dear,
By those that, through your fighting, you have made

Hast made thine enemies?
Your enemies?

ANTONIO
                    Orsino, noble sir,
        Orsino, noble sir,

Be pleased that I shake off these names you give me: 70
        Be happy that I'm not those things you call me.

Antonio never yet was thief or pirate,
        I never was a pirate nor a thief,

Though I confess, on base and ground enough,
        Though, I confess, on solid grounds, I was

Orsino's enemy. A witchcraft drew me hither:
        Your enemy. Deception brought me here.

That most ingrateful boy there by your side,
        That most ungrateful boy that stands beside you

From the rude sea's enraged and foamy mouth   75
        I rescued from tempestuous rough seas.

Did I redeem; a wreck past hope he was:
        I saved him; he had no chance of survival.

His life I gave him and did thereto add
        I gave him life and then I gave my love

My love, without retention or restraint,
        Without commitment or an obligation,

All his in dedication; for his sake
        And dedicated everything to him.

Did I expose myself, pure for his love,   80
        For him, and out of love, I risked it all

Into the danger of this adverse town;
        By coming to this dangerous, hostile town;

Drew to defend him when he was beset:
        I intervened, defending him from onslaught;

Where being apprehended, his false cunning,
        At that point, when arrested, his deception—

Not meaning to partake with me in danger,
        Not wanting to engage in danger with me—

Taught him to face me out of his acquaintance,   85
        Made him deny he knew of who I was,

And grew a twenty years removed thing
        Implying we'd not met in twenty years,

While one would wink; denied me mine own purse,
In the blink of an eye; he kept my wallet

Which I had recommended to his use
That I'd just recommended that he use

Not half an hour before.
Just half-an-hour ago.

VIOLA

How can this be?   90
How can this be?

DUKE ORSINO
When came he to this town?
When did you come to town?

ANTONIO
To-day, my lord; and for three months before,
Today, my lord; and for the past three months,

No interim, not a minute's vacancy,
Without a single moment spent apart,

Both day and night did we keep company.
Each day and night we've spent the time together.

[ENTER OLIVIA AND ATTENDANTS]

DUKE ORSINO
Here comes the countess: now heaven walks on earth.   95
Here comes the Countess. Heaven walks on earth!

But for thee, fellow; fellow, thy words are madness:
But as for you, boy, all your words are madness.

Three months this youth hath tended upon me;
This youth has worked for me the past three months.

But more of that anon. Take him aside.
I'll deal with you anon. Take him away.

OLIVIA
What would my lord, but that he may not have,
What do you want, my lord, except for that

Wherein Olivia may seem serviceable?   100
That I won't offer? Can I be of service?

Cesario, you do not keep promise with me.
Cesario, you broke your promise to me.

VIOLA
Madam!
Madam?

DUKE ORSINO
Gracious Olivia,--
Gracious Olivia...

OLIVIA
What do you say, Cesario? Good my lord,--
Cesario, what are you saying? Crikey!

VIOLA
My lord would speak; my duty hushes me.   105
My lord would like to speak; I must be quiet.

OLIVIA
If it be aught to the old tune, my lord,
My lord, if you repeat that same old story,

It is as fat and fulsome to mine ear
It's just the same damnation on my ears

As howling after music.
As howling after music.

DUKE ORSINO
                              Still so cruel?
You're still mean!

OLIVIA
Still so constant, lord.   110
I haven't changed.

DUKE ORSINO
What, to perverseness? You uncivil lady,
Not changed from being rude? You horrid lady;

To whose ingrate and unauspicious altars
I came to your unthankful, stony soul

My soul the faithfull'st offerings hath breathed out
With offerings of love so overwhelming

That e'er devotion tendered! What shall I do?
No one had offered more. What should I do?

OLIVIA
Even what it please my lord, that shall become him.   115
Do what you like, my lord, to flatter you.

DUKE ORSINO

Why should I not, had I the heart to do it,
Why shouldn't I, if I've the heart to do it—

Like to the Egyptian thief at point of death,
Like that Egyptian, dying, killed his wife—

Kill what I love?--A savage jealousy
Destroy what I adore? For savage envy

That sometimes savours nobly. But hear me this:
Is often dignified. But hear me out:

Since you to non-regardance cast my faith,   *120*
Since you've rejected all the love I've offered,

And that I partly know the instrument
And that I partly understand the cause

That screws me from my true place in your favour,
That stops my rightful place within your heart,

Live you the marble-breasted tyrant still;
I'll leave you to your stony-hearted torture.

But this your minion, whom I know you love,
But this, your sweetie, whom I know you love,

And whom, by heaven I swear, I tender dearly,   *125*
But whom, I swear, I also care about,

Him will I tear out of that cruel eye,
I will remove from your corrupting view

Where he sits crowned in his master's spite.
Where he sits now, against my better wishes.

Come, boy, with me; my thoughts are ripe in mischief:
Come on now, boy. My thoughts are truly awful.

I'll sacrifice the lamb that I do love,
I'll sacrifice this lamb that I do love

To spite a raven's heart within a dove.   *130*
To hurt a dirty heart within a dove.

VIOLA

And I, most jocund, apt and willingly,
And I would willingly, without a doubt,

To do you rest, a thousand deaths would die.
Succumb a thousand times to help you out.

OLIVIA
Where goes Cesario?
Cesario, where are you going?

VIOLA
After him I love
To him

More than I love these eyes, more than my life,   *135*
I love, more than I love my eyes or life,

More, by all mores, than e'er I shall love wife.
And more than I can ever love a wife.

If I do feign, you witnesses above
If I am lying, angels from above

Punish my life for tainting of my love!
Punish me now for cheating with my love.

OLIVIA
Ay me, detested! How am I beguiled!
Oh no, I'm hated! I've been cheated on!

VIOLA
Who does beguile you? Who does do you wrong?   *140*
Who's cheated on you? Who has done you wrong?

OLIVIA
Hast thou forgot thyself? Is it so long?
Have forgotten who you are so soon?

Call forth the holy father.
Go get the priest.

DUKE ORSINO
                    Come, away!
          Come on, let's go!

OLIVIA
Whither, my lord? Cesario, husband, stay.
Where to? Stay here, Cesario, my husband.

DUKE ORSINO
Husband!   *145*
Husband?

OLIVIA
          Ay, husband: can he that deny?
          Yes, husband. Will he deny that?

DUKE ORSINO
Her husband, sirrah!
Are you her husband, fella?

VIOLA
No, my lord, not I.
No, I'm not!

OLIVIA
Alas, it is the baseness of thy fear
Oh dear, it's just the fact that you are scared

That makes thee strangle thy propriety: *150*
That makes you hide the person that you are.

Fear not, Cesario; take thy fortunes up;
But don't be scared, Cesario. You're lucky.

Be that thou know'st thou art, and then thou art
Be who you know you are, for then you are

As great as that thou fear'st.
As great as what you fear.

[ENTER PRIEST]

O, welcome, father!
Oh, welcome father.

Father, I charge thee, by thy reverence,   *155*
Father, I ask, with your devout observance,

Here to unfold, though lately we intended
To tell these people here—though we intended

To keep in darkness what occasion now
To keep a secret what we're now obliged

Reveals before 'tis ripe, what thou dost know
To tell before we wanted—what you know

Hath newly passed between this youth and me.
What just occurred between this youth and me.

PRIEST
A contract of eternal bond of love,   *160*
A contract of eternal bonding love,

Confirmed by mutual joinder of your hands,
Confirmed my mutual joining of the hands,

Attested by the holy close of lips,
And sealed together with a holy kiss,

Strengthened by interchangement of your rings;
And strengthened by exchanging wedding rings,

And all the ceremony of this compact
And all the ceremony of a marriage

Sealed in my function, by my testimony: 165
Confirmed, as is my duty, verified;

Since when, my watch hath told me, toward my grave
And all this happened, as my watch confirms,

I have travelled but two hours.
Less than two hours ago.

DUKE ORSINO
O thou dissembling cub! What wilt thou be
You cheating, cunning fox-cub! What will you be

When time hath sowed a grizzle on thy case?
When time has turned you grey and made you old?

Or will not else thy craft so quickly grow, 170
Perhaps you'll get so good at your deceit,

That thine own trip shall be thine overthrow?
You'll cause your downfall, tripping on your feet;

Farewell, and take her; but direct thy feet
Goodbye, start walking, you can take her then

Where thou and I henceforth may never meet.
Where you and I will never meet again.

VIOLA
My lord, I do protest--
My lord, I must protest...!

OLIVIA
                           O, do not swear! 175
                          Leave grievance spared,

Hold little faith, though thou hast too much fear.
And keep the faith you have, although you're scared.

[ENTER SIR ANDREW]

SIR ANDREW
For the love of God, a surgeon! Send one presently
For love of God, I need to find a surgeon!

to Sir Toby.
Send one immediately out to Sir Toby.

OLIVIA
What's the matter?
What's the matter?

SIR ANDREW
He has broke my head across and has given Sir Toby   *180*
He cracked my head, and left Sir Toby with

a bloody coxcomb too: for the love of God,
a bloody head as well. For love of God,

your help! I had rather than forty pound I were at home.
we need your help! I'd give forty pounds to be home.

OLIVIA
Who has done this, Sir Andrew?
Sir Andrew, who has done this?

SIR ANDREW
The count's gentleman, one Cesario: we took him for
That servant to the Count, Cesario.

a coward, but he's the very devil incardinate.   *185*
We thought he was a coward; he's a monster!

DUKE ORSINO
My gentleman, Cesario?
My gentleman Cesario?

SIR ANDREW
'Od's lifelings, here he is! You broke my head
Good God, he's over there! You smashed my head

for nothing; and that that I did, I was set on to do't
for nothing; what I did do, I was told to

by Sir Toby.
by Sir Toby.

VIOLA
Why do you speak to me? I never hurt you: *190*
Why do you speak to me? I never hurt you.

You drew your sword upon me without cause;
You drew your sword to fight me without reason

But I bespoke you fair, and hurt you not.
But I was courteous and didn't hurt you.

SIR ANDREW

If a bloody coxcomb be a hurt, you have hurt me:
My bloody head is hurting, so you hurt me.

I think you set nothing by a bloody coxcomb.
I think you think a bloody head is nothing.

[ENTER SIR TOBY BELCH AND CLOWN]

Here comes Sir Toby halting; you shall hear more: 195
Here comes Sir Toby, limping. He'll say more.

but if he had not been in drink, he would have
If he had not been drunk, he would have fought you

tickled you othergates than he did.
far more effectively than how he did.

DUKE ORSINO

How now, gentleman! How is't with you?
What's up, good sir? How are you doing now?

SIR TOBY BELCH

That's all one: has hurt me, and there's the end
Oh, never mind. He hurt me, that's the truth.

on't. Sot, didst see Dick surgeon, sot?   200
Fool, have you visited Dick Surgeon yet?

CLOWN

O, he's drunk, Sir Toby, an hour agone; his eyes
I saw him drunk an hour ago, Sir Toby;

were set at eight i' the morning.
he hasn't moved his eyes since eight this morning.

SIR TOBY BELCH

Then he's a rogue, and a passy measures panyn:
Then he's a twerp, all staggering about.

I hate a drunken rogue.
I hate a drunken twerp.

OLIVIA

Away with him! Who hath made this havoc with them?   205
Take them away! Who brought this trouble on them?

SIR ANDREW

I'll help you, Sir Toby, because well be dressed together.
I'll help, Sir Toby. We'll be bandaged up together.

SIR TOBY BELCH
Will you help? An ass-head and a coxcomb and a
How will you help? You're just a clot,

knave, a thin-faced knave, a gull!
a fool, a simple-minded idiot.

OLIVIA
Get him to bed, and let his hurt be looked to.
Put him to bed, and let his wounds be looked at.

[EXEUNT CLOWN, FABIAN, SIR TOBY BELCH, AND SIR ANDREW]

[ENTER SEBASTIAN]

SEBASTIAN
I am sorry, madam, I have hurt your kinsman: *210*
I'm sorry, madam, I have hurt your uncle,

But, had it been the brother of my blood,
But even if he'd been my real brother,

I must have done no less with wit and safety.
I would have had to do the same for safety.

You throw a strange regard upon me, and by that
You're looking at me strangely, and by that

I do perceive it hath offended you:
I must assume that I've offended you.

Pardon me, sweet one, even for the vows   *215*
Forgive me, sweet heart, in the name of marriage

We made each other but so late ago.
We swore to one another earlier.

DUKE ORSINO
One face, one voice, one habit, and two persons,
One face. One Voice. One manner. But two people!

A natural perspective, that is and is not!
This has to be an optical illusion!

SEBASTIAN
Antonio, O my dear Antonio!
Antonio! Oh my dearest friend, Antonio!

How have the hours racked and tortured me,   *220*
It has been torturous for many hours

Since I have lost thee!
Since I lost track of you!

ANTONIO
Sebastian are you?
Is that really you, Sebastian?

SEBASTIAN
Fear'st thou that, Antonio?
Why do you doubt the fact, Antonio?

ANTONIO
How have you made division of yourself?
Have you split up and made yourself a clone?

An apple, cleft in two, is not more twin   225
An apple split in half is not more similar

Than these two creatures. Which is Sebastian?
Than these two people. Which one is Sebastian?

OLIVIA
Most wonderful!
This is amazing!

SEBASTIAN
Do I stand there? I never had a brother;
Is that me over there? I have no brother,

Nor can there be that deity in my nature,
And I don't have divine ability

Of here and every where. I had a sister,   230
To be in more than one place at a time.

Whom the blind waves and surges have devoured.
I had a sister who was lost at sea.

Of charity, what kin are you to me?
In goodness, tell me how we are related?

What countryman? What name? What parentage?
Where are you from? Your name? Who are your parents?

VIOLA
Of Messaline: Sebastian was my father;
From Messaline. My father was Sebastian.

Such a Sebastian was my brother too,   235
I had a brother called Sebastian too.

So went he suited to his watery tomb:
He drowned wearing the same attire as you.

If spirits can assume both form and suit
If spirits reappear in shape and costume,

You come to fright us.
You've come to scare us all.

SEBASTIAN

A spirit I am indeed;
My soul's a spirit,

But am in that dimension grossly clad   240
But I am wrapped within this larger body

Which from the womb I did participate.
That I've had since the day that I was born.

Were you a woman, as the rest goes even,
And if you were a woman, all things equal,

I should my tears let fall upon your cheek,
I'd let my sobbing tears run down your face

And say 'Thrice-welcome, drowned Viola!'
And say three times, "oh welcome, drowned Viola".

VIOLA

My father had a mole upon his brow.   245
My father had a mole upon his forehead.

SEBASTIAN

And so had mine.
And so did mine.

VIOLA

And died that day when Viola from her birth
And died that day that would have been Viola's

Had numbered thirteen years.
thirteenth birthday.

SEBASTIAN

O, that record is lively in my soul!
Oh, I remember that day very well!

He finished indeed his mortal act   250
He did indeed give out his final breath

That day that made my sister thirteen years.
The day my sister turned thirteen years old.

VIOLA

If nothing lets to make us happy both
If nothing gets between our happiness

But this my masculine usurped attire,
But this deceptive masculine attire,

Do not embrace me till each circumstance
Do not embrace me yet, until all proof

Of place, time, fortune, do cohere and jump   255
Of place and time and fortune all align

That I am Viola: which to confirm,
To show I am Viola; to confirm,

I'll bring you to a captain in this town,
I'll take you to a captain in the town

Where lie my maiden weeds; by whose gentle help
Where I have left my women's clothes; he helped

I was preserved to serve this noble count.
To save my life so I could serve the Count.

All the occurrence of my fortune since   260
And, since then, everything that has occurred

Hath been between this lady and this lord.
Has been between this lady and this lord.

SEBASTIAN
[To OLIVIA]

So comes it, lady, you have been mistook:
And so, my lady, you have been mistaken:

But nature to her bias drew in that.
But nature led you on to one like me.

You would have been contracted to a maid;
You almost nearly wed a virgin lady;

Nor are you therein, by my life, deceived,   265
But that is not entirely deception,

You are betrothed both to a maid and man.
For you are married to a virgin man.

DUKE ORSINO

Be not amazed; right noble is his blood.
Don't look so shocked; he's come from decent stock.

If this be so, as yet the glass seems true,
If true, as this here mirror-image claims,

I shall have share in this most happy wreck.
I'll share in this good fortune of the shipwreck.

[To VIOLA]

Boy, thou hast said to me a thousand times   270
Boy, you have said a thousand times to me

Thou never shouldst love woman like to me.
That you could not love women as you love me.

VIOLA

And all those sayings will I overswear;
And I will swear those words over again,

And those swearings keep as true in soul
And keep those promises within my soul,

As doth that orbed continent the fire
Just like the burning sun keeps promises

That severs day from night.   275
To split the night from day.

DUKE ORSINO

Give me thy hand;
Give me your hand,

And let me see thee in thy woman's weeds.
And let me see you in your woman's clothes.

VIOLA

The captain that did bring me first on shore
The Captain who first brought me onto shore

Hath my maid's garments: he upon some action
Has all my clothes. He has been charged and he's

Is now in durance, at Malvolio's suit,   280
Imprisoned at Malvolio's behest,

A gentleman, and follower of my lady's.
A gentleman and servant to my lady.

OLIVIA

He shall enlarge him: fetch Malvolio hither:
He'll set him free. Go fetch Malvolio.

[RE-ENTER CLOWN WITH A LETTER, AND FABIAN]

And yet, alas, now I remember me,
Oh, deary me, I've only just remembered

181

They say, poor gentleman, he's much distract.
They say that poor old man has gone insane.

A most extracting frenzy of mine own   285
For all my own distractions and concerns

From my remembrance clearly banished his.
Made me forget my memory of him.

How does he, sirrah?
How is he, fool?

CLOWN
Truly, madam, he holds Belzebub at the staves's end as
Well, truly, ma'am, he's holding off the devil

well as a man in his case may do: has here writ a
as well as someone can in his position.

letter to you; I should have given't you to-day   290
He's written you a note; I meant to give it

morning, but as a madman's epistles are no gospels,
to you this morning. But, as madman's notes

so it skills not much when they are delivered.
are not the gospel, it's fine if they're late.

OLIVIA
Open't, and read it.
Open it and read it.

CLOWN
Look then to be well edified when the fool delivers
You'll be enlightened when the fool has read

the madman.   295
the words the madman wrote.

[Reads]
'By the Lord, madam,'--
"By the Lord, madam..."

OLIVIA
How now! Art thou mad?
What's wrong with you? Are you completely mad?

CLOWN
No, madam, I do but read madness: an your ladyship
No, madam, but these words are mad. And if you

182

will have it as it ought to be, you must allow Vox.
want to hear it right, I must use crazy tones.

OLIVIA
Prithee, read i' thy right wits.   *300*
Just read it normally.

CLOWN
So I do, madonna; but to read his right wits is to
I am, madonna; reading normally

read thus: therefore perpend, my princess, and give ear.
means reading just like him. So listen up.

OLIVIA
[To FABIAN]
Read it you, sirrah.
You read it, sir.

FABIAN
[Reads]
'By the Lord, madam, you wrong me, and the
"By God, madam, you've wronged me, and I will

world shall know it: though you have put me into   *305*
tell everyone. Though you have locked me up

darkness and given your drunken cousin rule over
in darkness, letting your drunk cousin rule

me, yet have I the benefit of my senses as well as
over me, I have retained my senses

your ladyship. I have your own letter that induced
as good as yours. I have the letter from you

me to the semblance I put on; with the which I doubt
that led to my behaviour; with this letter,

not but to do myself much right, or you much shame.   *310*
I'll prove that I am right and bring you shame.

Think of me as you please. I leave my duty a little
I don't care what you think of me. I'll leave

unthought of and speak out of my injury.
my duties and tell you how you have hurt me.

THE MADLY-USED MALVOLIO.'
The one that you've abused, Malvolio."

OLIVIA
Did he write this?
Did he write this?

CLOWN
Ay, madam.   *315*
Yes, madam.

DUKE ORSINO
This savours not much of distraction.
Those words do not imply he is insane.

OLIVIA
See him delivered, Fabian; bring him hither.
Go get him Fabian, have him released.

[EXIT FABIAN]

My lord so please you, these things further thought on,
My lord, when you have thought this through, I hope

To think me as well a sister as a wife,
You'll love me just as much a sister as

One day shall crown the alliance on't, so please you,   *320*
You'd love a wife. One day you will be wed,

Here at my house and at my proper cost.
So do it here and I will pay for it.

DUKE ORSINO
Madam, I am most apt to embrace your offer.
Madam, I gratefully accept your offer.

[To VIOLA]
Your master quits you; and for your service done him,
Your master sets you free; for what you've done,

So much against the mettle of your sex,
Against inherent nature of a lady

So far beneath your soft and tender breeding,   *325*
And far beneath the status you were born to,

And since you called me master for so long,
And since you called me master for so long,

Here is my hand: you shall from this time be
I offer you my hand in marriage. From now,

Your master's mistress.
You'll be your master's mistress.

OLIVIA
A sister! You are she.
You're going to be my sister!

[RE-ENTER FABIAN, WITH MALVOLIO]

DUKE ORSINO
Is this the madman?   330
Is this the madman?

OLIVIA
                              Ay, my lord, this same.
                    Oh yes, my lord. This is the chap.

How now, Malvolio!
How are you, Malvolio?

MALVOLIO
Madam, you have done me wrong,
You've done me wrong, madam,

Notorious wrong.
A terrible injustice.

OLIVIA
                              Have I, Malvolio? No.   335
               Have I, Malvolio? I do not think so.

MALVOLIO
Lady, you have. Pray you, peruse that letter.
You have, my lady. Just peruse that letter;

You must not now deny it is your hand:
You can't deny that's not the way you write.

Write from it, if you can, in hand or phrase;
See if you can write differently than that

Or say 'tis not your seal, nor your invention:
Or say that's not your seal, or your creation.

You can say none of this: well, grant it then   340
You can say none of that. Admit it now,

And tell me, in the modesty of honour,
And tell me honestly, as is your honour,

185

Why you have given me such clear lights of favour,
Why you gave indications that you liked me?

Bade me come smiling and cross-gartered to you,
Why make me smile, and wear cross-gartered laces,

To put on yellow stockings and to frown
And put on yellow stockings; made me frown

Upon Sir Toby and the lighter people;   *345*
Upon Sir Toby and the common people?

And, acting this in an obedient hope,
And, when I followed this with keen obedience,

Why have you suffered me to be imprisoned,
Why did you let me suffer in the jail,

Kept in a dark house, visited by the priest,
Kept in the dark with visits by a priest,

And made the most notorious geck and gull
And made me be the world's worst idiot

That e'er invention played on? Tell me why.   *350*
Who's fallen for a trick? Do tell me why!

OLIVIA
Alas, Malvolio, this is not my writing,
Malvolio, oh dear! It's not my writing,

Though, I confess, much like the character
Though I admit it is quite similar.

But out of question 'tis Maria's hand.
But this, without a doubt's, Maria's hand.

And now I do bethink me, it was she
And now I think about it, it was her

First told me thou wast mad; then camest in smiling,   *355*
Who told me first you're mad; you came in smiling

And in such forms which here were presupposed
And dressed up in the clothes that are described

Upon thee in the letter. Prithee, be content:
For you within this letter. But, don't worry.

This practise hath most shrewdly passed upon thee;
This trick has been conducted shrewdly on you.

But when we know the grounds and authors of it,
But when we know the reasons and the culprits,

Thou shalt be both the plaintiff and the judge   *360*
   You'll be the prosecution and the judge

Of thine own cause.
   Of your own case.

FABIAN
                Good madam, hear me speak,
                Good madam, hear me out,

And let no quarrel nor no brawl to come
   And let's not have a fight or some debate

Taint the condition of this present hour,
   To spoil the happy times we're having now,

Which I have wondered at. In hope it shall not,   *365*
   Which I'm amazed at. Hoping that it won't,

Most freely I confess, myself and Toby
   I must confess Sir Toby and myself

Set this device against Malvolio here,
   Set up this prank against Malvolio,

Upon some stubborn and uncourteous parts
   Because of arrogant and rude behaviour

We had conceived against him: Maria writ
   Where he offended us. Maria wrote

The letter at Sir Toby's great importance;   *370*
   The letter at Sir Toby's instigation,

In recompense whereof he hath married her.
   And in return for that, he married her.

How with a sportful malice it was followed,
   It was intended as a bit of fun

May rather pluck on laughter than revenge;
   To incite laughter rather than revenge,

If that the injuries be justly weighed
   And if we weigh offences of both sides,

That have on both sides passed.   *375*
   We'll see they're much the same.

OLIVIA
Alas, poor fool, how have they baffled thee!
   Oh dear, old fool, they proper hoodwinked you!

187

CLOWN
Why, 'some are born great, some achieve greatness,
Why, "some are born great, some achieve greatness

and some have greatness thrown upon them.'
and some have greatness thrown upon them."

I was one, sir, in this interlude; one Sir Topas, sir;
I was involved as well, sir, as Sir Topas,

but that's all one. 'By the Lord, fool, I am not mad.'   380
but that was all. "By God, fool, I'm not mad!"

But do you remember? 'Madam, why laugh you at such
But then recall you said, "Madam, why do you laugh

a barren rascal? An you smile not, he's gagged:'
at this unfunny twerp? If you don't laugh, he's lost for words."

and thus the whirligig of time brings in his revenges.
And so, what goes around will come around.

MALVOLIO
I'll be revenged on the whole pack of you.
I'll get revenge on every one of you!

[EXIT]

OLIVIA
He hath been most notoriously abused.   385
He has been quite appallingly mistreated.

DUKE ORSINO
Pursue him and entreat him to a peace:
Go after him and try to calm him down.

He hath not told us of the captain yet:
He's not yet told us of the jailed Captain.

When that is known and golden time convents,
When that is known, and we've the perfect time,

A solemn combination shall be made
We'll make a solemn vow and we'll be wed

Of our dear souls. Meantime, sweet sister,   390
To tie our souls together. Meanwhile, sister,

We will not part from hence. Cesario, come;
We will not leave. Cesario, come here,

For so you shall be, while you are a man;
For I'll still call you that whilst you're a man.

188

But when in other habits you are seen,
But when in women's clothing you are seen,

Orsino's mistress and his fancy's queen.
You'll be my mistress, and my gorgeous queen.

[EXEUNT ALL, EXCEPT CLOWN]

CLOWN
[Sings]
When that I was and a little tiny boy,   *395*
With hey, ho, the wind and the rain,
A foolish thing was but a toy,
For the rain it raineth every day.

But when I came to man's estate,
With hey, ho, the wind and the rain,   *400*
'Gainst knaves and thieves men shut their gate,
For the rain it raineth every day.

But when I came, alas, to wive,
With hey, ho, the wind and the rain,
By swaggering could I never thrive,   *405*
For the rain it raineth every day.

But when I came unto my beds,
With hey, ho, the wind and the rain,
With tosspots still had drunken heads,
For the rain it raineth every day.   *410*

A great while ago the world begun,
With hey, ho, the wind and the rain,
But that's all one, our play is done,
And we'll strive to please you every day.

[HE EXITS.]

–END–

SHAKESPEARE RETOLD

For more online learning resources or to subscribe for updates from the Shakespeare Retold series, visit:

www.shakespeareretold.com

ABOUT THE AUTHOR

James Anthony is an award-winning, multi-genre author from London, England. With a keen eye, sharp wit, and poetic irreverence, he retold all 154 of Shakespeare's sonnets in modern verse, published by Penguin Random House in 2018. Described by Stephen Fry as 'a dazzling success,' he continues to retell the Bard's greatest plays in his popular 'Shakespeare Retold' series. When not tackling the Bard, Anthony is an offbeat travel writer, documenting his trips in his 'Slow Road' series, earning him the moniker the English Bill Bryson.

For more information on James Anthony's writing, visit:

www.james-anthony.com